# Praise for *The Book of Doing and*

"Barnet Bain's book gracefully conveys the thrill and discipline of the creative process. It will stretch you in unexpected ways that can unlock your creative heart."

—Geneen Roth, author of *Women Food and God* and *Lost and Found*

"This is quite simply the best book on creativity I've ever read. It is an eloquent theory of where the creative spark 'lives' and how best to access it, a complete toolkit for igniting your own creative potential, and a master class in the power of living life without a discernible compass. Follow its siren call, abandon the path of certainty, and learn to 'live on magic.' Consider this a course in creative miracles—your own."

—Lynne McTaggart, internationally bestselling author of *The Field*, *The Intention Experiment*, and *The Bond*

"Bain authentically demonstrates that 'BEING' with the right attitude puts your aptitude on steroids, so that you'll be active in 'DOING' for your success."

—Peter Guber, chairman of Mandalay Entertainment, co-owner of the Los Angeles Dodgers, and author of *Tell to Win—Connect, Persuade, and Triumph with the Hidden Power of Story*

"A glorious guide into our own possibility, into and past our blocks, to our true liberated being. Barnet Bain, a highly creative and innovative artist, helps us to unleash our gifts, talents, and vision. Bain starts with the premise that we each have a passion, a unique calling, and, if found, it helps us to live far more fully. Bain then gives us reason to believe in ourselves, and with some helpful steps, to realize our true nature, our calling!"

—Lisa Miller, PhD, professor and director of clinical psychology, Columbia University, author of *The Spiritual Child*

"Bain masterfully leads us to activate our creativity, innovation, passion, and purpose. Be bold. Explore this book and expand your imagination."

—Mark Van Ness, founder, *Real Leaders Magazine*

"Barnet Bain is devoted to manifesting creativity in a way that not only gives his life purpose but brings meaning and hope to the lives of others. With this book, he reveals to us how we can do the very same thing no matter our age, education, culture, or experience. Put simply, if you want your life to count in ways you've previously only dreamed of you owe it to yourself to read this book!"

—Ivan Misner, PhD, *New York Times* bestselling author of *Masters of Networking*, and Founder of BNI®

"With brilliant clarity, delightful humor, and deep insight, Barnet Bain reveals in *The Book of Doing and Being* how everyone can unlock their inner potential for creativity and make their dreams come true. I highly recommend it."

—John Gray, PhD, author of *Men Are from
Mars, Women Are from Venus*

"In this ode to the power of being, creativity, flow, and essence, Barnet Bain teaches us how to access our forgotten self so that we may live to our highest potential. Insightful, practical, and deeply compelling!"

—Dr. Shefali Tsabary, *New York Times* bestselling
author of *The Conscious Parent*

"No need to wait any longer for inspiration to strike or for the Muse to arrive in order to be creative. *The Book of Doing and Being* eloquently presents a treasury of creativity methods that you can use at any time."

—Zhena Muzyka, author of *Life by the Cup* and
founder of Zhena's Gypsy Tea Company

"*The Book of Doing and Being* is the 'how to' manual you have been waiting for! With enlightening wisdom Barnet Bain empowers us to ignite creativity and address the road blocks we encounter along the way."

—Kelly McNelis, founder of Women For One

"*The Book of Doing and Being* can be the catalyst to your next greatest creations, projects, and life's journeys. Barnet has found the most eloquent and experiential way of awaking in us and drawing from our souls the very energy required to illuminate and electrify this planet with an unparalleled creative force."

—Lisa Nichols, *New York Times* bestselling author of
*No Matter What*, featured teacher in *The Secret*

"If you haven't yet experienced the delight of attending one of Barnet Bain's workshops, this book will introduce you to a singular creative force: YOU. Experience your self as a spontaneous wellspring of fresh ideas, and put them into immediate action. Barnet will ignite your creative fire."

—Stephen Josephs, EdD, author of *Dragons at Work*

"If you think you are creative, you are. Even if you don't think you are creative, you still are. Either way, reading this book is an illuminating journey of discovery that offers to usher you into a state of aliveness through your full self-expression in day-to-day life."

—Stewart Emery, coauthor of *Success Built to Last*

# THE BOOK

## OF

# DOING

## AND

# BEING

*Rediscovering Creativity in*
*Life, Love, and Work*

## Barnet Bain

**ATRIA** PAPERBACK

NEW YORK  LONDON  TORONTO  SYDNEY  NEW DELHI

NOTE TO READERS: Names of some of the people portrayed in this book have been changed.

**ATRIA** PAPERBACK
An Imprint of Simon & Schuster, Inc.
1230 Avenue of the Americas
New York, NY 10020

First Atria Paperback edition July 2015

**ATRIA** PAPERBACK and colophon are trademarks of Simon & Schuster, Inc.

For information about special discounts for bulk purchases, please contact Simon & Schuster Special Sales at 1-866-506-1949 or business@simonandschuster.com.

The Simon & Schuster Speakers Bureau can bring authors to your live event. For more information or to book an event, contact the Simon & Schuster Speakers Bureau at 1-866-248-3049 or visit our website at www.simonspeakers.com.

Designed by Esther Paradelo

Manufactured in the United States of America

10   9   8   7   6   5   4   3   2

Library of Congress Cataloging-in-Publication Data
Bain, Barnet.
  The book of doing and being : rediscovering creativity in life, love, and work / Barnet Bain.
     pages  cm
  Includes index.
Summary: "How to unlock your most creative self"—Provided by publisher.
1. Creative ability.  2. Creative ability in business  I. Title.
  BF408.B333  2015
  153.3'5—dc23

                         2014047583

ISBN 978-1-4767-8546-2
ISBN 978-1-4767-8547-9 (ebook)

FOR SANDI

# CONTENTS

# CONTENTS

CONTENTS

## CHAPTER 15
*The Uncommon Senses: Rediscovering Intuition*

## CHAPTER 16

## CHAPTER 17

## CHAPTER 18

# INTRODUCTION

When I was growing up in Canada, my dad was a butcher and my mom was a housewife. Around the dinner table, the conversation would often include talk about customers at my dad's shop, neighbors, friends, and others in our community. On occasion, the conversation would turn to Grégoire, a wedding photographer and quite a good painter with a small studio in town. The scent of photo-developing chemicals and espresso followed Grégoire wherever he went. With his scarves, long hair, and French accent, he had a romantic mystique about him. My parents always referred to him as a "freelancer"—a word that packed a lot of meaning. Most important, it meant that he had no reliable income, therefore, no safety. It was both terrifying and exciting to hear about Grégoire and how he couldn't rely on the world for money, validation, or a certain future.

Nothing about the way I was raised had any rapport with the freewheeling idea of being a freelancer, and yet I have become one. I have created a blueprint that is sufficiently differentiated from the framework of my beginnings—I created it, in part, by stepping beyond the bounds of *structured imagining*, which is something I'll teach you how to do in this book. And while I know there are no guarantees—no promise of assured good outcomes in my career, finances, health, love, or anything else—there is also no turning back. Even if I wanted to turn back, the line to the anchor has been cut. I'm too far from the shore, and there is no safe harbor to return to. I have to *create* safety, trusting that safety found within myself will show up in my experience of the world. Most of the time, I am on tranquil seas, and yet sometimes it gets stormy, tempestuous. I hit moments of stress and fear that call me to return to the trance, but I can't do it. I can only live on magic, fueled by my passion and commitment to the creative life.

When you seek out and explore creativity, as you will do by working with the exercises and practices in this book, it leads to an individualization from your original blueprint, which can be both exhilarating and unnerving at the same time. Instead of reacting to or rebelling against a framework that has been preset by others, you get to harvest what works of it and set about consciously creating the life you desire.

No matter what your vocation, you come to realize that *life* is a freelance affair and you no longer take anything for granted, whether it's a paycheck, a marriage vow, or your health and well-being. You discover that none of these is outside of you. You can't put them in a vault to accumulate interest and guarantee a particular future. Everything that matters to you comes from an inner reservoir that is always available in the present moment.

When you know that your whole life is a creative act, you begin to take responsibility for every piece of it. And claiming 100 percent responsibility makes everything crystal clear. You can see that each one of us is a freelancer, regardless of job title. You know that each of us is the writer and director of our own unforgettable life story.

That knowing is a fundamental shift in perception—a transformation. It happens when you are intimate enough with your past to be able to create an original framework that is yours alone, one that is as distinctive to you as your fingerprints. Living from the inside out, every facet of your life is freelance, designed by your own hand. You are a free agent. *You are free.*

## THE PRESENT IS NOT THE RESULT OF THE PAST

Every act is a creative act. A relationship, a business, a screenplay, a dance, an art form, a reality—everything we know and everything we love is a constellation of creative acts.

Ensconced in our favorite corner of a restaurant where we frequently meet, my friend Barbara and I were fully engaged in a conversation about the creative life. We asked each other, What is a creative life? What does it look like? What does it feel like? How is it expressed? We were overflowing with ideas, many of which had made their way onto the large piece of white paper that covered the tablecloth, creating a mind-map of our thoughts. I'm grateful we did that because I have since referred to my piece of the map many times, drawing great inspiration from it and even adding new threads as they come to me.

At the center of our conversation was the idea that we are always evolving, individually and collectively. And if we are willing to be surprised by the next thing—the next creative impulse, the next idea that excites us, the next experience that moves us—then we are living a creative life. This dynamic is true for everyone, whether a stay-at-home parent, a CEO, a musician, a retail salesperson, an actor, a social media manager, or a monk. It cannot be otherwise.

The present does not have to be a continuation of the past.

Creatively redefining and reimagining our lives is an ongoing and perhaps inevitable conversation for Barbara and me to have. Barbara is Barbara Marx Hubbard, the celebrated futurist and eloquent communicator of evolutionary potential. I am a screenwriter and film producer. So she and I are both storytellers who share a passion for chronicling and understanding the unfolding human drama in which each of us has a vital role to play.

Over the past thirty-five years, my career has followed a particular trajectory that made itself clear early on. Reflected in the movies *What Dreams May Come, Homeless to Harvard, The Celestine Prophecy,* and others, that focus has to do with the mechanics of creativity itself, especially its connection to consciousness. Creativity is a *relationship* you nurture—must nurture, or life ceases to delight and surprise. If you offer yourself to creativity, it will seize you; shower you with wonders. For several years, I have spoken of this on film sets, in workshops, and at events around the country. But as we sat together that afternoon,

Barbara said, "People have wonderful things to share, but most of us don't realize that we are actors on the stage of *history*—and every actor needs a coach at some point."

Right there, as she spoke those words, I knew the time was right for this book. Although my passion for creating films continues unabated, I realized in that moment that my larger role is that of attuning others to their part of the play, their part of the story that life is telling on a grand scale.

But in this great play, none of us has a script. We make up our parts as we go. So, in order to know what we want to create and *why*, we need a deeper understanding of ourselves.

## CREATIVITY AS A STATE OF MIND

When we say, "I want to create something," what we are really saying is, "I want to change things. I want to make something more beautiful . . . or more safe or more efficient or more sustainable." All creativity starts with that desire to have impact, and the ownership of that desire is everything. In that sense, conscious creativity, perhaps more than anything else, requires an admission of a particular state of mind.

There is a little movie-set parable that says it all.

The tour guide stops his trolley on the Universal Studios back lot. Three craftsmen are hammering and sawing and painting away. The guide says, "Hey, what are you all doing?" The first one says, "What do you think? I'm painting a wall." The second one says, "I'm doing okay; I'm making a living." Then, covered from head to toe in paint, the third one looks up, and she says, "I am making our summer blockbuster." She was the one who had a sense of the bigger picture and fully owned her part as a creator.

Over my desk hangs a hand-painted card by the writer J. Stone that says, "The most visible creators I know of are those artists whose medium is life itself. They neither paint nor sculpt. Their medium is *being*. Whatever their presence touches has increased life."

That is the potential this book can serve to unlock or amplify, tapping great reservoirs of positive energy that you can use all kinds of ways, whether toward the completion of a creative project or in the way you approach your next conversation. Whatever you choose to create, at the root is always the opportunity to become the artist of being *alive*.

## THE CALL OF YOUR REAL WORK

I had a wonderful dog for many years whose name was Siri. When Siri would drag me around on our walks, he would focus all his senses on these invisible trails, like ley lines emanating from the earth, signaling new and exhilarating possibilities just around the next bend. With his nose to the ground, he would eagerly chase these mysterious trails. As I watched him, Siri seemed an expression of pure creative force—entirely unconscious, of course; instinctive but with his nose to the call, ever alert to the grand evolutionary creative turning of things. Here was this beautiful little dog who was, in his own four-legged way, on a hero's journey. Locked on to the trail with no guarantee as to where he would end up, but ready to be transformed by life.

When I am fully engaged in creative work, when my nose is to the trail and I am locked on to the call, I can *feel* it. And when I lose connection with that impulse and go off course, I feel that, too.

This book is designed to help you find *your* trails and to follow them. These are the trails that lead to your deepest fulfillment as a creator. You have a purpose, a mission, and a calling that is uniquely your own. The Sufi poet Rumi goes directly to the heart of the matter in his discourse on finding and claiming your real work:

> There is one thing in this world that must never be forgotten. If you were to forget all else, but did not forget that, then you would have no reason to worry. But if you performed and remembered everything else, yet forgot that one thing, then you would have done nothing whatsoever.

It's as if a king sent you to the country to carry out a specific task. If you go and accomplish a hundred other tasks, but do not perform that particular task, then it is as though you performed nothing at all. So everyone comes into this world for a particular task, and that is their purpose. If they do not perform it, then they will have done nothing.

It is as if you were given a sword of priceless Indian steel, and you were to treat it as a butcher's knife for cutting up putrid meat. . . . Or it is like taking a solid gold bowl to cook turnips in, when a single grain of that gold could buy a hundred pots. Or it is as if you took a Damascene dagger of the finest temper to hang a broken gourd from, saying, "I am making good use of it . . . I am not letting this dagger go to waste."

From *Discourses of Rumi, Discourse Four,*
original translation by A. J. Arberry

Your real work, of course, isn't confined to your job title or description alone. It might *include* your professional vocation, but it does not start or stop there.

If you are unclear at the moment as to what your real work is or if you feel that the signals of your creative impulses are scrambled, the principles and practices in this book will assist you in gaining clarity. And if you feel creatively blocked, stalled along the shoulder of the creative highway, it will help you to jump-start your creative engine.

Your creative capacity is greater than you know. Even if you are already prolific and productive, you can become even more so. You will find your real work in your values and what matters most to you; in your creative ambitions; in your skills and abilities; and, of course, in your strengths, talents, and gifts. As you clarify these facets of your creativity throughout the book, simultaneously you will be building the courage and commitment to express them.

## THE EMOTIONAL POWER THAT FUELS CREATIVITY

What does it take to tend to every part of your life more creatively? To lock on to the creative call? To harness a personal creativity that can touch the whole world? It requires becoming connected to your passion, to your excitement, and to your enthusiasm. From that connection comes the desire to contribute and to make change.

It also requires that you check under the hood, explore the subtle nature of creativity. Energy is more powerful than the thing being created, no matter what that "artifact" might be. Whether the creation is a nonprofit organization, a book of poetry, a friendship, or a new perception, it is the *resonance* of that creation that we are really seeking—the frequency, which comes from what we think, what we feel, and what we express through our emotions. In the pages of this book, you will learn how to tune in to your emotions with ease and creatively shift frequencies at will, not as a reaction to extrinsic factors but intentionally, from the inside out.

## HOW TO WORK WITH THIS BOOK

The more inspired and innovative you are, the better off the world is. I offer this book as both a practical support structure and a reminder that your creative dreams matter—whatever they may be. If you already know what those dreams are, this book will help you to fulfill them. And if you aren't clear about your creative dreams right now, you will be soon.

The framework of the book is a diverse selection of exercises—techniques, processes, rituals, and creative tools. In addition to the exercises in each chapter, you will also find others in the spaces between certain chapters. Each one can augment the power of your discovery process. Together, these exercises form the latticework on which your creativity can grow and flourish. Whether you like big, blank pages or the architecture of lines, I recommend getting your favorite kind of notebook for this exploration—your journal of doing and being.

Starting in the first chapter, you will find that all the exercises are designed to activate creativity by jostling the connections of your subconscious and conscious minds. They jiggle the strings of your usual ways of thinking, feeling, and perceiving so that something new can occur. This is important because our conscious mind is always looking to string things together. We are devoted to the straight line, with logical and reasonable connections and explanations, but creativity comes from a "place" that is entirely unconstrained by any lines—that is where we are going.

Imagine there are two kinds of lives: the life we are *given* and the life we *create*. The life we are given is the one that is shown to us by our parents and caregivers. They demonstrate how to live, love, and relate to the world. They make the distinctions that determine the boundaries between what is practical and realistic versus what is quixotic and dreamy. We are not specifically schooled in these. We adopt them automatically.

For my parents' generation, life was laid out. You got a job, raised a family, received the gold watch, and retired. That linear trajectory is not the life that most of us lead today. Cause does not lead to effect the same way it did in the past. Nowadays, we frequently find ourselves in unpredictable chaos, moving with both excitement and trepidation through various jobs, vocations, and relationships. While we enjoy the ability to reinvent ourselves at will, most of us occasionally long for the kind of predictability our parents had.

Nevertheless, we can venture beyond the life we are given to a life we create, unbound by hand-me-down conventions modeled for us by others. *A created life looks different.* Friends and colleagues who work with these practices maintain longevity and aliveness no matter what their chronological age is. They focus more on where they are going than where they have been, and they always seem to have all the luck—though luck has nothing to do with it.

## The Power of Practice

As you use these exercises with consistency, you establish a creativity practice. Practice is like the guardrails on the side of the highway that keep you on the road. Practice keeps you focused and heading toward your desired destination. The attention and commitment to practice allows your creativity to persist and not to dissipate. Without practice, our creative thoughts, insights, and ambitions seem to float away like tumbleweed in the wind—nice ideas that never go anywhere. Practice grounds us; it allows our ideas and ambitions to take root and grow.

## Making Time for Creativity

Set a formal practice time every day. When you wake up in the morning you brush your teeth and comb your hair; that is a practice. Without that practice, your teeth would fall quickly into a bad state. Apply the same diligence and commitment to your creativity practice. Find your own timing and cadence, but know that it is imperative that you honor your creativity in the same way that you honor your health and grooming.

Beyond simply setting aside time, you have to *create* time. Time does not exist unless you create it. Whenever we pursue a creative goal or endeavor with intentionality, with a closeness that generates a different kind of rapport with our experience, magic happens. We create time through the power of our intention and presence. Our grandmothers knew this when they used to say, "If you want something done, ask a busy person." They understood that busy people are passionate people. "Losing track of time" is a hallmark of passionate action. Time is an ally that can be as slow or fast as you need it to be.

When has this happened to you? You are passionate about putting in your tulips, or writing copy for your new website. When you look up from your passion, hours have flown by. You have temporarily suspended your relationship to the clock, and productivity is the result.

Your relationship with time is much more fluid and dynamic than you think it is. You can consciously develop a new kind of partnership with the clock through intention and presence born of passion.

## Your Creative Workspace

What separates the real creator from the wannabe? Commitment. Set up your creative workspace so that it reminds you of your commitment every time you step into it. Simple additions and attention to detail can put you in the mood to create. Here are some ideas to consider:

- Play music you love.
- Light a candle.
- Add flowers or a living plant.
- Declutter and organize your space.
- Open a window to let some fresh air move through.
- Add a new lamp to shed a warm light on your creative work.
- Choose an object for your creative space that represents your commitment to your creativity, something personally meaningful to you. It could be a stone, a crystal, a piece of art, or a photo of someone who inspires your creativity.

## Your Creative Helpmate

Treat this book as a helpmate and resource. You can read it cover to cover or drop in on any page for a boost, like a creative *I Ching*, the classic Chinese text for gaining clarity through intuitive investigations. These pages are a distillation of everything I know about creativity; together they comprise an expansive tool kit of creativity principles and techniques.

I cannot claim every one of the tools in this kit as my own, although they have added immeasurably to my creative life. I have learned from many fabulous teachers along the way. For those tools and techniques derived from people whose names are mentioned and for those whose source I no longer remember, I am grateful.

I hope that, by working with this material, you will find your own creative process less mysterious than you thought it was and more productive and fulfilling than you ever imagined.

# CHAPTER 1

## *Freedom from Conditioning*

*Creativity is a type of learning process where the teacher
and pupil are located in the same individual.*
—BEATRIX POTTER

Creativity matters to everyone, but conventional wisdom holds that creativity is the special gift of poets, painters, sculptors, musicians, and other culturally ordained elites and that there are limited outlets for creative energy.

My view is that *everything* is a process of creativity. Maybe you're not interested in creating a comedy routine, a symphony, or an off-Broadway play, but you probably have a desire to create loving relationships, a vibrantly healthy lifestyle, or perhaps a business as an outlet for your skills and interests. Business is one of the primary forms of creative expression in our culture today. Although you might feel blocked or uninspired from time to time, you can't really stop the flow of this force. Each of us is always a creator, and we are all creating all the time. When we let in the implications of that, it changes everything. We discover that *everything* matters. What we think, what we feel, what we believe, what we say, what we choose, and what we do—these are the instruments we use to create and shape our lives.

*Everything is a process of creativity.
We are all creating all the time.*

## BECOMING A SOLUTION-MAKER

Creativity is worth our attention, as well, for reasons that reach beyond our own lives. We all sense that we are living in a world that is changing at lightning speed. Some days it seems as if we are in the third quarter of an endless game and hopelessly behind. To meet the challenges of a world that is becoming new, to effectively address problems that appear to have too few solutions, creativity must be awakened. We need innovative responses and new skills. From business and politics to the way we tend to our personal lives, we need to stretch our imaginations beyond outmoded practices.

This requires an education in creativity itself. Opening our eyes to new potentials, creativity gives us the fuel to transcend conditioned ways of thinking, feeling, and behaving. Nothing and no one is left behind when we lead creatively.

Fortunately, we can all become "weapons of mass creation." It is the birthright of every human being. There are solutions in the making, and some of them may very well come from *you*.

First, it is important to find out how we have gotten ourselves into a creative straitjacket . . . and what it takes to get out of it.

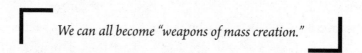

*We can all become "weapons of mass creation."*

## A PSYCHOLOGICAL VIEW OF CREATIVITY

A common assumption about creativity is that you must have *conflict* for it to emerge. I am as responsible as anyone for propagating this notion, along with most of my entertainment industry friends and colleagues. In particular, comedians and comics say, "If I don't have my neuroses to feed on, then I'm afraid my creativity will dry up."

Freud had a big hand in building this thought structure, but it reduces us to mere vehicles of expression of our neuroses. Not long after

Freud, Carl Jung said that creativity is the expression of a duality of functions: it's both personal and an expression of the underlying archetypes that reflect our collective human experience. Archetypes are universal patterns of energy that transcend time and place and contain the raw power at the heart of all our stories of love and courage. In the popular mind, certain archetypes are widely recognized, such as the lover, hero, warrior, judge, as well as the artist. Jung's view affirms the individuality of the artist, yet recognizes that he or she is also an instrument in service of more powerful forces.

Abraham Maslow placed creativity in the top tier of his hierarchy of needs, after all other needs have been met—after shelter, safety, security, love, belonging, and self-esteem. Inside his model, creativity exists within the domain of self-actualization, a need that one can't understand until all the other needs have been fully mastered. I understand why Maslow would prioritize hunting down your next meal before going to the dance around the bonfire. But it's my view that going to the dance *first* might bring the creative inspiration needed for a fruitful hunt. *Engaging your creative urges is causative*; it creates more flow in relation to meeting your needs. Dance itself is a creative and generative act. Only through creative acts can we rise above our conditioning.

That is a really big one to let in.

> *Only through creative acts can we rise above our conditioning.*

Picasso said that creativity is, first of all, an act of destruction. Creativity first shatters our conditioning, our unexamined beliefs, and our assumptions, which naturally exposes how much we take for granted.

I often look at how much I take for granted, how much I am a product of my conditioning. I would like to ask you to do the same.

If you were to draw me an alien from another dimension, you would probably create something wonderful and weird, but it would likely be vaguely humanoid, like something from the bar scene in *Star Wars*. More than 99 percent of the time, that is what happens. And while there is nothing wrong with that imagery, why not draw something we wouldn't recognize as a life form at all?

## STRUCTURED IMAGINING

The reason we tend to draw inside the lines is because we have inherited those lines and perspectives. We are products of our families, peer groups, schools, entertainment streams, and religions. We are shaped by the movies, TV shows, songs, news bites, stories, and art forms offered to us by other people—expressions of the tragedies and triumphs that seem to dictate the reach of our imagination. Some call this *structured imagining*, which is our unconscious adoption of other people's thinking, feeling, beliefs, and values. We are mostly unaware that we have acquired a hand-me-down worldview.

If structured imagining is a major block to conscious creativity, how can we ever create anything beyond our conditioning? First, we need to understand the power of conditioning. The following demonstration will make the point.

Right now, wherever you are sitting, lift your right foot a few inches off the ground and then start moving it in a clockwise circle. At the same time as you're doing that, raise your right hand and draw a number six in the air.

What happened? Your right foot switched directions, didn't it? Try it again. The reversal will happen every time!

## BRAIN PATTERNING—OLD AND NEW

The implications of this exercise are that our habituated patterns of thinking, feeling, and behaving become a part of our brain chemistry.

As we repeatedly activate the same neural pathways, we reinforce our current understanding of creativity and of ourselves.

In business settings, this can be seen in the creative framework that makes up a company culture. Although corporations pride themselves on having cultures, they are often, though not always, based on long-standing values and ingrained approaches to facing change.

A good illustration of this comes out of post–World War II Japan. As Japanese manufacturers turned their attention from military goods to civilian goods, they focused on improving not only their products but every organizational process as well. They effectively reshaped the manufacturing of electronics and cars and served as an example that led to the introduction of Japanese-style manufacturing in the United States. The core message of what became known as the Quality Revolution was that, by improving quality, companies would decrease expenses and increase productivity and market share. Although this philosophy was an unprecedented advance over previous patterns of thinking and responding to change, it was nonetheless an improvement of past practices rather than a quantum leap forward. It still existed inside the framework of what we already know, and what we already know is only a fraction of what is possible.

The jump to altogether new territory can be seen in the shift from snail mail to email, for instance, or in the difference between manufacturing using metal lathes and 3-D printing. These are not simply creative improvements, better versions of what was. They are disruptive advances that we call *innovations*.

Innovation is the discovery of anything that is beyond the horizon of what is—whether a new invention, a company, a marriage, or a self. We can get wedged inside structured imagining and miss out on innovation because the patterns of structured imagining are hardwired into our circuitry, but there are many things we can do to positively alter our brain chemistry. Throughout this book, as you work with the raw materials of your thoughts, beliefs, choices, decisions, attitudes, feelings, and emotions, you will be rewiring your creative neuronet. You will be working with each of these in fun and engaging ways, through discussion, processes, and practice. When we consciously make a new habit through practice, new brain patterning follows and old patterns begin to atrophy.

In his book *Outliers: The Story of Success*, author Malcolm Gladwell describes what he calls the 10,000-Hour Rule. Gladwell makes the case that it takes a lot of practice to master a skill, from the Beatles performing live in Germany amassing more than 10,000 hours of playing time over a period of four years, to an adolescent Bill Gates gaining access to a high school computer and spending more than 10,000 hours learning the art of programming. Any parent knows the rapport that children have with their digital devices, having surpassed 10,000 hours with ease, dwarfing the skill level of their parents.

But more important than the specific number of hours devoted to an activity is *consistency*. Committed practice develops mastery. Whether learning to tie your shoes, pilot a plane, or communicate effectively in relationships, after a point of repetition new habits and new brain circuits allow you to do these things with excellence. You develop a new talent or skill by focusing attention on it and establishing a practice around it. This is one of the great secrets of all creative processes, and a major purpose behind each exercise in this book.

## Taking the Lid Off Structured Imagining— A Self-Inquiry Practice

The more that we as creators become aware of the limitations of our structured imagining, the more power and choice we have to move beyond it. Just as we can't sell a house that we don't own, we can't be free of structured imagining until we become aware that we have been structured by it.

This awareness is the first critical piece of opening to your fuller potential. Paying attention to your thoughts and feelings is the starting place for expanding this awareness.

The following self-inquiry practice can be used any time you have a sense that conditioned modes of thinking and feeling are limiting your creative drive or inspiration.

**STEP 1**: Bring to mind a creative project or goal that you are either working on now or planning to begin in the near future.

**STEP 2**: Are you experiencing any challenging or difficult thoughts and feelings related to this project or goal? Are these thoughts and feelings stopping you from taking action or diminishing your confidence? If so, briefly describe them.

_____

_____

_____

_____

_____

**STEP 3**: Spend ten to fifteen minutes reflecting on the following questions and writing your answers in your journal:
- Are these thoughts and feelings hand-me-downs, or are they originating with me?
- Am I being loyal to thoughts, feelings, and beliefs that I have outgrown?
- Am I willing to give up old perceptions, feelings, and attitudes when something more valuable shows up?

This practice will remind you to respond creatively rather than out of habit. It can empower you to realize that you have choice where, before, no choices seemed to be available. Not long ago, I received a call from a colleague with whom I was involved in a writing project. We had been facing challenges that threatened to derail the project. My knee-jerk reaction was to avoid his call, but after remembering this practice, I realized that my concerns about the situation were hand-me-downs from the past. Was I willing to give them up? Yes, I was. I picked up the phone and dealt with the situation quickly, which led to a positive outcome.

If you decide to keep certain hand-me-downs, it's not necessarily a problem. There is nothing good or bad about making that choice; just make sure it works for you. Also, you will be more attuned to the "something more valuable" from Step 3 as you become clearer about your *values* in the chapters ahead. One of the fundamental truths of creativity is that we can't be valuable creators unless we have clear values. Paying attention to your values on an ongoing basis increases your creative intelligence.

## CHAPTER 2

# Into the Wilds of Creative Imagining

*Do not seek the because—in love there is no because,*
*no reason, no explanation, no solutions.*
**—ANAÏS NIN, *HENRY AND JUNE***

I was in line at my neighborhood store to get a coffee. Next to me stood a man whose wife was buying a couple of kiddie pails for the beach. He told me they were from Seattle but had just driven down to Los Angeles from Santa Barbara. He referenced a tragedy that had taken place the previous week: a young man had gone on a rampage near the University of California campus at Santa Barbara, wounding thirteen people and killing six others.

I thought he had said that a friend's child was one of those slain in the attack.

"No, it was my child," he said.

"We're going to take her ashes and scatter them in the Pacific . . . I don't know why I'm telling you this," he continued, "but it helps to say it."

I was unglued. I saw my conscious mind grasping for a logical framework to make sense of what this grieving father had told me. But below the level of my rational mind, I *felt* something else. I knew something.

His pain and my pain are connected. His ability to love and mine are connected.

Below my logic and reason, something more true in me had been triggered—an unfamiliar intelligence.

*There is nothing logical about it.*

Our creative lives are always a back-and-forth between what makes sense to the logical mind and something more, beyond the borderline of structured imagination.

## THE IQ EFFECT—OUR LOVE AFFAIR
## WITH LOGIC AND REASON

Intelligence Quotient, or IQ, is a numerical score based on standardized tests that attempt to measure human intelligence by focusing on our cognitive abilities. Yet we know that there is much more to intelligence than verbal and mathematical abilities that are measured by fixed and graded tests. Although we put ourselves through the rigors of such testing, we don't really like to be reduced to a few numbers.

The poet Walt Whitman wrote, "I am large, I contain multitudes."

I believe that the multitudes he was referring to are *intelligences*—a plurality of capacities; dimensions of self that are diverse, colorful, and sometimes paradoxical in nature.

Besides logic and reason (the favored tools of conventional wisdom), other kinds of intelligence include emotional, empathetic, musical, athletic, intuitive, and social. Some forms of intelligence relate to aspects of consciousness: the child, adolescent, and adult self; the higher self; the future self; the mystical self; the subconscious; the unconscious; and unity consciousness.

Most often we live in the world as a tightly defined, limited "me"— someone who is bound by conditioned ideas that get expressed as:

"This is how I think."

"This is what I often feel."

"This is what I normally do."

"This is who I must be."

But when we relate to ourselves as a synthesis of many intelligences, we can begin to sense the awesome creative power that is available. We are much more than the sum of our parts. Yet understanding that can be difficult because of our loyalty to logic and reason. The rational mind can create a false boundary between our understanding and the wildness and freedom of our imagination.

## FROM IQ TO CQ—INTRODUCING THE CREATIVITY QUOTIENT

IQ is one measure of our ability to process our experience through logic and reason, but other creative tools exist beyond our cognitive abilities. Those capacities include *sensing, being,* and *knowing,* which I refer to as CQ—our Creativity Quotient. These are gifts and talents we possess that are keys to a broader ability to conceive and perceive—whether or not we are familiar with them.

Your Creativity Quotient is fluid and dynamic, flowing and ever changing. CQ describes your personal relationship with "the first principles of things," which is the primordial creativity of higher consciousness and spirituality.

The following quiz will help you recognize the territory of your Creativity Quotient.

## What Would You Do or Be?— The Creativity Quotient Quiz

Consider the following questions, and check the box with the answer that most closely depicts your style of response. While you will likely relate to both answers, choose the one that is most instinctive.

You learn that an unexpected financial windfall may come your way.
☐ **A:** You think of all the reasons it will or will not happen.
☐ **B:** You feel the wonder of having resources show up in surprising ways.

You are at a show where a magician performs a stunning feat of magic.

☐ **A:** You try to figure out the trick.

☐ **B:** You get lost in the spell of the magic.

You find a tiny flower in the desert.

☐ **A:** You wonder how it survived the scorching sun.

☐ **B:** You admire its fragile beauty.

You are blindfolded and given a food to taste and a scent to smell.

☐ **A:** You try to identify them.

☐ **B:** You experience them sensually.

A friend or family member tells you about a personal crisis.

☐ **A:** You look for solutions to fix their problem.

☐ **B:** You listen attentively with empathy.

You are pondering your future and where you want to be in five years.

☐ **A:** You write down your goals and the action steps you will need to take in order to achieve them.

☐ **B:** You dream about what you will be doing and with whom; you imagine how you want to feel.

You are invited to collaborate on a project that would stretch you creatively, requiring you to utilize new tools and processes, thereby stepping beyond your comfort zone.

☐ **A:** You weigh the pros and cons and think about the repercussions if you fail.

☐ **B:** You sit quietly and tune in to your feelings before proceeding.

The nightly news program reports a new uprising of violence in another country.

☐ **A:** You push the mute button on the remote control and go raid the refrigerator.

☐ **B:** You notice that your stomach is in a knot and take a breath to release the tension.

You wake up in the morning with a sore throat, achy muscles, and feeling like you haven't slept a wink.

☐ **A:** You recount the people you've been around over the past few days and try to figure out where you caught the bug.

☐ **B:** You know you've been overdoing it and stressed, and sense that you need a break.

Out of the blue, your sweetheart puts his or her arms around you and gives you a warm embrace.

☐ **A:** You wonder what he or she wants.

☐ **B:** You take it in, and feel your heart soften.

*Tally your answers:* Note the total number of As and Bs. Your B answers provide a clear picture of perceiving and relating that points toward CQ.

## THE COST OF IGNORING
## OUR CREATIVE INTELLIGENCE

Tragic things occur when we dismiss creative intelligence in favor of logic and reason alone. Our personal imagination collapses, for one thing, and hope and vision atrophy. Vision is what creates the expansive boundaries of what is possible and hope is the bridge that can take us there.

We rely solely on conventional wisdom, societal norms, and popular culture to provide us with our understanding of the world. Instead of creative imagination, we participate in a kind of groupthink. Our dreams atrophy. We lose the confidence to imagine successful outcomes, and set our sights and expectations lower and lower. Dogma takes the place of authentic dialogue. Tune in to talk radio and you'll have the picture. There is no room for nuance or complexity. Pundits speak from a polarized sense of the issues, and no one is spacious enough or present enough to listen to another point of view. In all of this, we lose a sense of compassion, understanding, and empathy. This lack of imagination is at the root of the great crises in our world today. When our personal imagination collapses and our creative intelligence withers on the vine, we are left clinging to positions that leave no room for innovation and discovery.

> *Develop your creative intelligence in order to*
> *build your intelligence beyond logic and reason.*

## INTO A NEW WORLD

We are at a crossroads. We can survive and thrive by learning to step from an outmoded system that values absolutes, predictable outcomes, and guarantees into a more powerful, fluid one. This is at the heart of why we develop our creative intelligence—in order to build the *relationship* with aspects of our intelligence beyond logic and reason.

We don't lose sight of logic and reason, but simultaneously transcend and include them. We make a quantum leap, like jumping from a game of checkers to 3-D chess.

Some people in the public eye point to their inner life as an important source of creative inspiration. Ohio Congressman Tim Ryan says that meditation is a part of his daily routine. It's not logical, but his internal practices help him to see his mind as an ally. Actor Angelina Jolie talks about experiencing meditative moments in everyday things. In a 2012 NBA play-off game, star basketball player LeBron James famously took a time-out to refocus and shift his attention to his inner state.

That is creative intelligence in action.

### Priming the Pump of Your Creative Imagination

Find a place where you can sit quietly for a few minutes. Settle in and take a few slow, deep breaths. Bring to mind a project that you are either in the midst of right now or one that you would like to initiate in the future, perhaps a dream project.

Take a few moments to close your eyes and allow your project to fully enter into your awareness. The first part of this exercise is an opportunity to creatively interact with your project through the senses:

**Smell.** Smell can stir memory, including the memory of creative dreams that might have been seeded in your consciousness long ago. If your project had a smell or fragrance, what would you imagine it might be? Would it smell like wildflowers? Freshly printed pages of a new book? Exotic spices from a distant land? The subtle fragrance of your spouse's perfume or cologne?

**Touch.** If you could physically touch your project, what would it feel like? What are its textural qualities? Smooth, bumpy, or silky? Is it layered and thick or paper-thin? Is it warm, cool, or moist?

**Taste.** If you could taste your project, what flavors or taste sensations would you experience? Put your tongue on it. Is it spicy? Sweet? Does it wake you up like a squeeze of lemon? Does it have one distinct flavor, or is it a balance of many?

**Sound.** If your project had a sound, what would it be? Is it a melody? A rustling breeze? A crashing wave? A symphonic crescendo? A hum? Is the sound loud or soft?

## PART II

You are going to partner with your subconscious mind as we invite aspects of your innate intelligence to weigh in on the creation of your project. As you activate various thoughts, feelings, and images, your subconscious will make no distinctions at all as to whether they are real or imagined. It is ALL real to the subconscious. This is because only the conscious mind is bound by logic, which gives context to our experiences. It filters and compartmentalizes reality and provides meaning and a sense of control. The subconscious, on the other hand, collects *everything*; it remembers the restaurant menu you saw when you were ten years old, the shape and texture of the rock you skipped across the surface of a lake when you were eight, every license plate you have ever seen, in order—every detail you have ever absorbed. It would be overwhelming to retain that all at once, like Raymond, Dustin Hoffman's character in *Rain Man*, who lived with an extraordinary condition called savant syndrome where vast amounts of subconscious data were available to him at all times.

As you proceed through this exercise, keep in mind that the most powerful creative partnership you can make is the one with your subconscious mind. As the gatekeeper to all our creative power, you want to make an ally of it. Develop it, explore it, and commit to it with full awareness and intention.

Close your eyes again and imagine that your project is *already complete*. Consider it from the perspective of different aspects of yourself that are listed below—each is a unique expression of your creative intelligence. What do they want you to know or understand about your project and what led to its successful completion? Let yourself see a word, phrase, symbol, or image offered by some of your "multitudes."

Your confident self says: _____

Your accomplished self says: _____

Your abundant self says: _____

Your higher self says: _____

Your child self says: _____

Your analytical self (the keeper of your IQ) says: _____

Your feeling self (the keeper of your emotional intelligence) says:

_____

_____

Others aspects of your consciousness say: _____

As you write down your answers, trust the images, colors, sensations, feelings, ideas, and inspirations that come to you.

Engaging senses and invoking your imagination in this way can result in surprising payoffs. As I was workshopping a movie project based on Frances Hodgson Burnett's novel *The Secret Garden*, I discussed the project with Joan Scheckel, my directing coach, talking about how to establish one of the characters. Joan advised me to find music that conveyed the tone of the character as I wanted the actor to play it. Her powerful suggestion set off a small avalanche of ideas for me. Tuning in to the qualities of the character, I gathered music, as well as poetry, photographs, and images of artwork that conjured certain feelings. I found scents from natural oils that evoked certain emotions, and textiles that felt unique to the touch. I amassed a treasure trove that I brought to the actor. I didn't want to simply discuss my thoughts about the character. I wanted to create a sensory environment in which the actor could meet me to discover the character together. There is nothing logical about that.

If you give your creative projects to logic alone, it will diminish them. Don't settle for that.

# *Try This!*

## INTELLIGENCE QUOTIENT VERSUS CREATIVITY QUOTIENT—AN EXERCISE IN PERSPECTIVE

**STEP 1**: Choose an event that has taken place to describe from two different perspectives—IQ and CQ. For example, how would you describe the first lunar landing of Apollo 11 in 1969 or the first landing on Mars?

**STEP 2**: First describe the event through the lens of logic and reason, from IQ. Looking through the window of conditioned and structured thinking, what do you see? In the case of the lunar or Mars landings, you might see a great scientific accomplishment. You might see the many men and women who devoted countless hours of research and planning to make it happen.

**STEP 3**: Now describe it from CQ—from your creativity quotient. For instance, in the case of one of the space landings, a priest might view it as a miracle, an artist might view it as a landscape to be rendered in a painting, captured by texture and color, and a child might view it as a playground.

Allow yourself to tap into the many streams of thought and feeling through which you perceive and experience the world.

**CHAPTER 3**

# Foundational Creativity: Energies of Creation, Part I

*Our duty, as men and women, is to proceed*
*as if limits to our ability did not exist.*
*We are collaborators in creation.*
**—PIERRE TEILHARD DE CHARDIN**

There is something you want that drew you to this book. A goal. A dream. A desire. You would like to create something and you are looking for tools, techniques, and inspiration to support that desire. You might also be wresting with your personal version of the "if onlys."

If only I had an abundance of time.

If only I felt inspired instead of tired.

If only I had unwavering focus and concentration.

If only I had the right surroundings, a real creative space to work in.

If only I had the money to fund my project or to take a few months off from my job.

If only the stars would align and help propel me toward the fulfillment of my goal.

If you want to create something and you're not doing it, what stops you? While a lack of focus and time may be a problem for you, the real issue almost always stems from a misunderstanding of the energies of creation—the masculine and feminine energies that give rise to all *doing* and *being*.

## DIFFERENTIATING MASCULINE AND FEMININE QUALITIES—FROM DOING TO BEING

We all have both masculine and feminine energies, no matter what sex we are. Together the masculine energies and the feminine energies create All That Is. "Doing" and action characterize masculine energy. This is expressed outwardly in dynamic ways, but can act more subtly as well. Seeking understanding, for example, and finding meaning and significance are subtle expressions of the masculine principle. The masculine energy *makes* things—from pencils to skyscrapers to films. It builds, structures, orders, and files. The primordial urge to protect by providing for others and creating safety is a masculine quality, whereas the drive to protect through nurturing is a feminine quality.

"Being" characterizes feminine energy. The capacities to imagine and feel, and also the *receptivity* to imagination and feelings, are feminine. In a dance with the masculine, the feminine qualities include perception and conception. The essence of perception and conception is to be pregnant with the possibility of *all* possibilities—the *possibility* to act, the *possibility* to make things, the *possibility* to build, to write business proposals and books, to have friendships, to create anything at all. Intimately joined with the masculine, the feminine expresses the *ability* to act, the *ability to* create, the *ability* to manifest, to build, to bring order, etc. The gestalt of these feminine qualities is the primal desire and impulse of creativity itself.

So if there is something that you want to create and it's not happening, the lack and struggle are often symptomatic of the one *big* stumbling block to creativity. The real creative hitch, and this may surprise you, is chauvinism.

## CHAUVINISM AND ITS IMPACT ON CREATIVITY

The chauvinism I'm referring to is not a belief in the superiority or inferiority of either sex, but a systematic disorder that reinforces our structured imagining—the conditioned creativity that we explored earlier.

At its core, chauvinism is an elevation of will and action over imagination and feeling. Every time we value the masculine "doing" qualities over the feminine "being" qualities, chauvinism is at work. The qualities of the feminine are the primal creative energies. All creativity begins with the feminine—with the sense of possibility, with the desire to feel and to imagine, with the potential for bringing something into being. The feminine energy is the medium that holds the space out of which all things arise. We cannot become pregnant with the possibility of creation if, unbeknownst to us, we are harboring competition, anger, or hostility toward our innate feminine traits.

Today, men and women alike are overidentified with their masculine qualities. As a result, both sexes get trapped inside structured imagining. *When we prioritize doing over being, when we have the slightest bit of intolerance toward the feminine aspects of our nature, it shows up as pushback against the primal creative force.* Talk about a creative block. What ensues is a serious case of swimming upstream.

When feminine and masculine traits are allowed and encouraged to join together, they generate a powerful cocreative force.

## GAINING ACCESS TO CREATIVITY
## THROUGH OUR EMOTIONS

Emotions are the well of creativity for the feminine aspect within each of us. We gain access to our creative life *through* our emotions. If our well of emotions is shallow, when we throw in our bucket, we might come up empty and feel unclear, flat, or otherwise blocked. If our well is deep, we throw in a bucket and bring up an idea, insight, intuition, or other generative nugget that we need for our creative process.

In order to deepen your access to your feminine creative force, recognize that *all feelings occur in the body.* You can sense enthusiasm and excitement, for instance, as a thrill in the body. You may experience worthlessness or loneliness as a hollow feeling. However your feelings signal you, they are never experienced in the head.

For many years, what I used to call "feeling" was really obsessive thinking; mental anxiety rather than body feelings. Back then, I would have said I was feeling worry or fear or excitement. More accurately, I was focused on *thoughts* about worry, or fear, or excitement. I was "stuck in my head" and would stay there for long periods of time, ruminating over past events or concerns about the future.

One time, a close friend was ill. He was losing his sight in one eye, and I worried about his well-being because of what I knew about his past health issues and what I thought might happen next. I felt plenty of mental distress, but few embodied feelings. My mind ran off with all kinds of possibilities that existed purely in my imagination. My wife, Sandi, with her strong intuitive caring, sensed my distress and helped guide me to find some relief.

Inviting me to relax, she asked, "What are you feeling in your body?"

I wasn't aware of anything at first.

"I notice that you're barely breathing," she said.

She was right. I was breathing very shallowly. I took a few deep breaths, and as I felt the air filling my lungs and diaphragm, I suddenly realized that I breathe shallowly *most* of the time.

"Can you feel any part of your body now?" she asked.

I noticed tightness in my chest and neck, a few aches here and there. Breathing again, I felt some queasiness and sensed that the feeling in my stomach was connected to what was happening with my friend. That was a breakthrough moment as I began to discover that my feelings occur in my physical body—a foreign and exotic land that I hadn't explored much. As I sat quietly, feeling more open and present, it suddenly seemed strange to live in a body and not have rapport with it.

Chauvinism separates us from our feelings. As we reconnect to our bodily senses, we reorient ourselves to our feminine aspects and our feeling sense begins to come alive again. Creativity comes alive, too.

Each in our own way, we rediscover that emotions are our tools of expression, as chisels are to sculptors.

> *Emotions are our tools of expression,*
> *as chisels are to sculptors.*

## THE TWO PARTS TO CREATIVITY

There are two forces of creativity: *inspiration* and *action*.

Inspiration always comes as a gift from beyond—beyond what we already know, understand, and believe; beyond our current sense of ourselves; beyond our current expression of thoughts and feelings. It is a gift bestowed from aspects of ourselves that are, as yet, unknown to us.

Equal to inspiration are *will* and *action,* the "doing" part of us that is responsible for the technique, craft, and manifestation of our creativity. Will and action throw the piece of pottery, build the relationship, draw up the plans, and fund the start-up. In business, will and action turn on the lights and open the doors every day.

Will is often exercised through thinking and the cognitive abilities of the mental body. Inspiration may sometimes include mental processes, but it always involves feelings that we experience in the physical body.

The more in touch we are with our feelings, the more we are in touch with creativity.

## EROS—WHEN TWO BECOME ONE

The dynamic qualities of will and action come together with the receptive qualities of imagination, feeling, and being to form the foundation of creativity. As we bring together the feminine and masculine energies, we are calling on the archetypal generative force known as *Eros*. Eros breathes new life into our thoughts and feelings, arousing body, mind, and spirit. With that, we might experience flashes of intuition or the quiet joy that comes from reclaiming aspects of ourselves that we thought we had lost.

While searching for a metaphor to describe how the principles of creativity work, I had an intuition that I should look into something called Indra's net. I didn't know exactly what Indra's net was, except that it had something to do with Hinduism and Buddhism, and that in some way it conveyed interconnectedness. I googled it and found exactly the image I was hoping for: Over the palace of the great god Indra hung a glorious net that stretched infinitely in every direction. Inside each cross tie of the net was stitched a single glittering pearl. And in each of the infinite pearls of the net was the reflection of every other pearl, out through infinity.

The masculine *doing* energy—including will and action—reduces whole entities into component parts. It slices, dices, and parses as its natural function. Yet, as Indra's net illustrates, all things are both separate and connected at once. When we enter *being* states, we remember our connection to the infinite whole and gain access to it. In flashes of intuition, inhalations of primordial creativity without doing, we reach beyond the limits of structured imagining. We connect with the well.

This interplay of doing and being creates a field of connection and communication that requires no words, although words might be shared. It's an energy field that is palpable. Creation is a gift of Eros.

# *Try This!*

## JUMP-START A CREATIVE PROJECT

What would you like to create? A song, a book, a recipe, or a new way of behaving in your intimate relationship? What project would you like to jump-start? The following exercise is for you if . . .

You know what you want to create but need inspiration and motivation to restart your creative engine.

Or you don't know what you want to create right now, but you feel the creative fires stirring and want to identify a new project.

## JUMP-START A CREATIVE PROJECT— THE EXERCISE

### *Relax Your Mind*

Begin by relaxing your mind and body. Allow yourself to stop thinking for a few minutes. We're about to take a little trip beyond our structured imagining.

### *Random Selection (My Secret Weapon)*

Next, turn your attention away from everything you have been thinking about and doing up to this point. You're going to choose something completely arbitrary, plucking something right out of your immediate surroundings. This is a fun way to step off of the parched ground of structured imagining and get your creative juices flowing.

Below are some of the ways that I fish for information and inspiration. I encourage you to try as many of them as you wish and devise some of your own as well.

*Go to the eighth word on a random page of your thesaurus or dictionary. What do you see? Drainpipe? Daffodil? Filibuster?*

*Open to a section of the* Huffington Post *and count down to the thirteenth picture you find. What is that image of? A sports car? A movie star? A kitten?*

*Walk out your front door and find four things that contain the color orange. What is that fourth thing? A fruit tree? A bicycle? A fluorescent orange traffic cone?*

*Open a magazine to the tenth page. What is in the top-right corner? A diamond ring? A cloud? A slogan?*

*Search the general Jobs section of Craigslist. Count down to the twentieth listing. What service does that job provide? Customer service? Roto-Rooter? Copywriting? Insurance preparation?*

## MAKING THE LINKS—
## GENERATING NEW IDEAS

If you have already chosen a creative project, think about how this random selection (or selections) applies to your idea. Look for the links between your arbitrary selections and your project.

If you haven't chosen your creative project and are seeking clarity, look at your random selections to generate new ideas and new thinking. Which word, image, or symbol triggers an invigorating thought or an intriguing feeling?

In either case, give yourself permission to be imaginative with your interpretations. Try on different modes of thinking— go for literal thinking, lateral thinking, and opposite thinking. Try metaphors and similes. Look through the eyes of humor and other intelligences. Let your imagination trigger as many fresh connections and associations in your mind as possible, and follow where they lead you.

Many times the ideas that seem the most farfetched, the most outrageous, or the least pertinent to me, might offer the strongest creative kindling . . . the ignition that I have been waiting for.

## THE COMMITMENT OF TIME

Once you have identified a new project or gotten reinspired about a current one, the next important step is to create the *time*—to make time in your schedule to pursue your desired goal. Time is a fundamental aspect of the commitment that we make to our creative pursuits.

Taking your other time commitments into account, what does your ideal schedule for this project look like? Is it twenty minutes every day? One hour five days per week? One full day each week? Is it in the morning, afternoon, or evening? Play with the possibilities and then make a decision that you stick with. Make your time commitment inviolate.

## THE NEXT BEST STEP

You are almost there. Your creative jump-start requires one more decision, and it's all about *action*. It might be an action in the outer world, or it might be something internal. Perhaps you need to gather tangible resources or to access an internal resource, such as trust or faith. Maybe your next step involves making a phone call, scheduling a meeting, or cleaning off your desk. Whatever your next step may be, the most important thing is to follow through with it in a timely fashion, preferably within the next twenty-four hours.

Taking one more slow, deep breath, simply ask yourself the following question:

What is the next step for me to take?

_____

_____

_____

_____

_____

_____

_____

_____

# CHAPTER 4
## Creativity and the Body

*When you reach the end of what you should know,*
*you will be at the beginning of what you should sense.*
—KAHLIL GIBRAN

Your emotions are the well of your creativity. One of the greatest secrets to living a creatively vibrant life is to recognize that your feelings occur in the body and not in the head.

For me, this realization sank in on a trip to Bali. My wife, Sandi, and I were with a group of friends when we visited a temple where there was a healer. Sandi, always the most adventurous, was the first to sit with him. Wordlessly, he began to touch different sensitive pressure points on her body, then he told her that her mind was very passionate and alive, but her body was not so alive, not so happy. He asked her to smile. I looked over at her from a distance and saw her beaming. Then he asked her to *swallow her smile* so that her body could be as happy as her head.

After Sandi had "swallowed her smile," the healer touched the pressure points on her body again, which had been quite painful at the start of the session. Now these same pressure points didn't hurt at all. Sandi could *feel* that a connection had been made between her mind and body. Since then, I've adopted the smiling practice, too.

Not only do our feelings occur in the body and not in the head, but creativity itself is born in the body. In other words, the body is the home of our creativity.

Thoughts and feelings come together as the emotions that move through the body—moving us in countless ways to express what is alive within us. We speak, sing, pray, write, pirouette, strum, whisk, pluck, paste, click, and otherwise articulate the pulsations of life that come through us.

*The body is the home of our creativity.*

## Going to the Well—The Master Practice

The body-emotions-creativity link is crucial to living a creative life. I am indebted to Jeremy Whelan, the founder of the Mosaic Acting System, for this process I call Going to the Well, which is inspired by Jeremy's work. Designed to loosen the grip of structured imagination, this exercise will stir the embers of your creativity.

Most important, I want you to see, hear, and smell through the eyes, ears, and nose of your *heart*, the most trustworthy sensor you have.

The following guidelines will prepare you for the ten-step process.

*Set the Tone.* Create an atmosphere that welcomes your creativity and kindles your emotions. If you can, play a piece of music that you enjoy, light a candle, and turn off your cell phone. Take a slow, deep breath to bring your attention to the present moment.

*Choose One Emotion.* From the Vocabulary of Feelings list on page 36, choose one word—select the one that jumps off the page for you. This word will be the fulcrum for this practice, the point where feelings and thoughts are expressed as an emotion.

Given our conditioning, we can go into our heads when selecting and deciding on a word. We try to "figure things out." From there we assess, compare, and judge. We may intuitively connect with one word and then decide that there is a much better one in the next column. This is the way of logic and reason. This process, however, is an opportunity to remember that creative emotions are felt in the body, not in the head. Body associations are what we are interested in here rather than psychological associations.

Tune in to the first sensation that comes to you, like the first smell that tickles your brain (the smell of rain on asphalt on a hot summer day) and the first color that comes into your awareness (the brown of my omelet, which reminds me of rust on a car bumper). Be specific with your imagery. Rather than sensing or seeing "puppies," look again. Six-week-old cocker spaniel puppies might be napping at the feet of your imagination.

**Declare with Confidence.** As you proceed through this exercise, you will be connecting more fully with your emotion by discovering its weight, taste, texture, smell, color, sound, and symbols. Use this discovery as an opportunity to express your creative self with confidence. One potent way to do this is to make *declarative statements* rather than turning your imagery into metaphors. For example, say, "The sound of my jealousy *is* one hundred balloons popping," rather than, "The sound of my jealousy *is like* one hundred balloons popping." I don't want to know what it's *like*; I want to know what it *is*.

As you declaim what you are seeing and sensing in this way, you foster the confidence to express your emotions more honestly and fully.

You also begin to access a poetry of images and sensations that are alive in you—where a seemingly ordinary emotion becomes a portal through which magic starts to unfold.

**Time It—Three Minutes.** Read through the ten steps of the exercise the first time, before you answer the questions. Then you will be ready to choose your one emotion. Once you've done this, take a look at your clock and give yourself three minutes to do this practice. Set a timer if you like. You only need to write down one example for each category. Enjoy the experience of allowing yourself to flow easily from one step to the next, finding a rhythm that feels good to you.

## Going to the Well—The Worksheet

STEP 1: Choose One Emotion. When you find your one emotion in the following Vocabulary of Feelings list, feel into it with your body. Sense it through your heart, as we discussed above. Use the list as you would use the *I Ching*. Let it be arbitrary. Allow your finger to go round and round on the page. Close your eyes, and then stop. Wherever your finger lands, that is your word. That is the emotion you're going to work with. *Example: Resentment*

My emotion is:

_____

_____

**STEP 2**: The Definition of Your Emotion. Write down a brief definition of your emotion. It doesn't need to be a dictionary definition. Go freestyle. Let it flow from your stream of consciousness. *Example: Resentment is a corrosive feeling that I get when I decide that I am being treated badly.*

The definition of my emotion is:

_____

_____

_____

**STEP 3**: The Color of Your Emotion. Imagine the color of your emotion. Think expansively. Visualize the color wheels and palettes that you see on your computer screen. There are more than a million different color distinctions on a smart phone—a reminder that we can stretch beyond "blue" or "green" or "yellow." You can also describe the color beyond a one- or two-word name (for example, "It's the chartreuse and sunburst big-top tent from my day at the circus."). *Example: My resentment is the brown of an omelet.*

The color of my emotion is:

_____

_____

_____

**STEP 4**: The Weight of Your Emotion. Sense the weight of your emotion. The weight can be in standard measurements, such as pounds, ounces, or kilos, but don't limit yourself to those, either. Your creative imagination might sense the weight in surprising ways, such as "nine supertankers of feathers," or "two pillows of goose down." *Example: The weight of my resentment is seven bales of Hummers.*

The weight of my emotion is:

_____

_____

_____

**STEP 5**: The Taste of Your Emotion. Imagine the taste of your emotion. Your intuitive and uncensored "tongue" can be very descriptive. It might be the taste of crisp apple, dry cotton balls, or warm chicken fat. *Example: The taste of my resentment is liquid sunblock.*

The taste of my emotion is:

_____

_____

_____

**STEP 6**: The Texture and Feel of Your Emotion. Inwardly connect with the texture and feel of your emotion. Your emotion could have the texture of putting your hand in a tub of warm popcorn or the feel of icy snow resting on your eyelashes. As the "feel of my resentment" example below shows, the texture might not satisfy your logical mind, but you can trust it nonetheless. *Example: The feel of my resentment is having my leg slip in between satin sheets.*

The texture of my emotion is:

_____

_____

_____

**STEP 7**: The Symbol That Represents Your Emotion. A sigil is a symbol the subconscious mind uses as a continual prompt, encouraging it to work toward the delivery of a creative outcome. It's a metaphysical doodle, a scribble you draw with your own hand that holds meaning for you. It keeps the subconscious working on an outcome even when you're not consciously working on it. In that way, it's like a bug in your computer . . . only it's a really creative bug. *Example:*

The sigil that represents my emotion is:

**STEP 8**: The Smell of Your Emotion. Imagine the smell of your emotion. It could be a single aromatic note, a delicate fragrance, an acrid scent, or a strange and unexpected blend. Allow the smell to waft into your awareness. It could be lavender flowers and lemons; your grandfather's shaving cream and waffles. . . . *Example: The smell of my resentment is fresh-cut grass and spilled motor oil.*

The smell of my emotion is:

_____

_____

_____

**STEP 9**: The Sound of Your Emotion. Listen for the sound, hearing with the ears of your heart. The sound might be close, loud, distant. It could be one tone or an emotional quartet. It could be a fierce rainstorm beating on the roof or the breath of your sick uncle in your ear. *Example: The sound of my resentment is President John F. Kennedy giving his "Ask Not What Your Country Can Do for You" speech. This is the sound of my resentment because I have feelings of resentment around how that dream has not turned out.*

The sound of my emotion is:

_____

_____

_____

**STEP 10**: The Talisman That Represents Your Emotion. Functioning very much like a sigil, a talisman is an object found in nature or the physical world that you give meaning to consciously. It is a metaphor for your emotion that connects with your subconscious. It could be a river stone, a dog collar, a golden key, any object that tells the story of your emotion. *Example: The talisman of my resentment is an elephant's trunk.*

The talisman that represents my emotion is:

_____

_____

_____

*Note: If you want to mix things up, here is one way to play with your chosen word—your one emotion: Within a day or two, look up your word in a thesaurus and find another word that is a synonym. Run that new word through the ten-step process. You will be surprised to discover how closely related words can spark very different creative responses in you.*

This is a powerful practice for rewiring your brain, assisting you to become close and intimate with your emotional capacity. It will help you to both *identify with* your emotions and to *relate to* them. I encourage you to use this practice frequently; make a habit of it. I recommend doing it once a week for a time. Return to it regularly, especially when many things are happening at once and you want to stay closely connected to your emotional center.

## THE TOOLS: WORD AND IMAGES

*Vocabulary of Feelings*

| | | |
|---|---|---|
| adored | confused | fond |
| affectionate | contented | frazzled |
| afflicted | crazed | friendly |
| afraid | cruel | frustrated |
| amazed | defeated | fuming |
| angry | delighted | funereal |
| appalled | depressed | gleeful |
| appreciative | deranged | gloomy |
| apprehensive | devastated | grateful |
| aroused | discouraged | guilty |
| ashamed | disheartened | happy |
| astonished | dismayed | hateful |
| baffled | dispassionate | heartbroken |
| beaten | eager | horny |
| berserk | ecstatic | humble |
| bitter | embarrassed | humiliated |
| bored | embittered | hung-up |
| bouncy | enthusiastic | hysterical |
| calm | envious | inadequate |
| cantankerous | exasperated | incompetent |
| capable | exhilarated | indifferent |
| concerned | exposed | infatuated |
| conflicted | fearful | insecure |

insignificant
irritable
jazzed
jealous
jolly
joyful
jubilant
livid
lonely
loved
loving
merry
miserable
narcissistic
needed
negative
nervous
numb
overburdened
panicked
passionate

playful
proud
provoked
puzzled
quarrelsome
rattled
regretful
rejected
relaxed
resentful
reserved
sad
sarcastic
seething
sexy
shamed
sorry
startled
surprised
tearful
tender

terrified
thrilled
thunderstruck
trusting
uncertain
uncooperative
understood
unfeeling
unhappy
unloved
unsettled
uptight
vain
vindictive
wanted
warmhearted
weary
worthy
yearning
zealous
zestful

## REVIEWING YOUR WORKSHEET

Once you have gone through the ten steps of the worksheet and re-viewed your answers, I recommend that you read your list out loud. As you do this, remember that your emotions and feelings are experienced in your body, and place your attention there. Give your head a rest and notice the feelings, sensations, and images that emanate from different parts of your body.

When you come to the place where you describe your sigil, trace your drawing of it lightly with your fingertip as a way to integrate it into your body.

The following examples came from participants in my creativity programs who read their lists out loud to the group.

### Example #1

1. My emotion is trust.
2. The definition of my trust is something you have with another person.
3. The color of my trust is periwinkle blue.
4. The weight of my trust is a heavy wool blanket.
5. The taste of my trust is sour apple.
6. The texture of my trust is a rough, scratchy washcloth.
7. The sigil that represents my trust is a ripple, like a ripple in a pool of water.
8. The smell of my trust is the tang of an overripe apple.
9. The sound of my trust is the shriek of a high-pitched whistle.
10. The talisman that represents my trust is a brass skeleton key.

### Example #2

1. My emotion is puzzlement.
2. The definition of my puzzlement is a curiosity that encompasses confusion. It is open and delighted to discover what is hidden.

3. The color of my puzzlement is a kaleidoscope, a rainbow of cascading all-colors.
4. The weight of my puzzlement is a wicker basket full of daisies.
5. The taste of my puzzlement is cold gazpacho soup topped with fruit chunks and Honey Nut Cheerios.
6. The texture of my puzzlement is cotton balls made out of steel wool.
7. The sigil that represents my puzzlement is an upside-down tree growing out of the sky.
8. The smell of my puzzlement is a wet ostrich.
9. The sound of my puzzlement is a tuba that has gone flat.
10. The talisman that represents my puzzlement is the same kaleidoscope, in pieces.

Taking it further: Any time you use this exercise, you can return to your responses during the week. As you read through them again, sense how the pieces string together. Feel into them and do some journal writing to further unpack the one emotion.

## THE BODY'S POETRY

When you connect with your senses without an agenda to create any particular "thing" but simply to experience the body's creative aliveness, something magical happens. You will often be surprised by your senses when you invite them to express themselves authentically. Stringing your words and descriptions together as you have just done, they bounce, spin, and interact with one another in ways that are pure creativity.

The more you explore your creativity beyond the bounds of logic and reason in this way, you will begin to see that you are a poet. You may also be a journalist, a graphic designer, a mother of three, a loan officer, or a loan shark. But you are a poet, too.

Each of us is transformed into a Keats, a Dickinson, or a Rumi every time we tell the truth about what is alive inside us.

# *Try This!*

## PICASSO-ING—DRAWING YOUR SOLUTIONS

Structured imaginations always make creativity a matter of intellect—headtrips focused on doing. But the body has its own intelligence, which is focused on being. When we draw, dance, run, make love, we are introducing underutilized body intelligences into our creative process. By coming home to the body, we access creative awareness and embodied potentials that are beyond logic and reason.

*Preparation:* Select your art supplies. Find the paper you like. Choose the drawing tools that you enjoy—pens, colored pencils, pastels, crayons, markers, or a combination thereof.

STEP 1: Bring to mind a problem that you are having, whether big or small. Without getting mired in it, go ahead and see it, sense it, feel it.

STEP 2: With your paper and drawing tools, give yourself the freedom to address the problem with artful abandon. This drawing practice is most effective when you are doing it *abstractly*. In that way, you will be welcoming the unlimited resources of your imagination.

In no particular order . . .
- Draw your problem.
- Draw your feelings.
- Draw your desires.
- Draw your solution(s).

STEP 3: Make a commitment to yourself to act on the solution (or solutions) you have drawn.

## CHAPTER 5

# Creativity in Balance: Assessing Your Life Wheel

*Life isn't about finding yourself. Life is about creating yourself.*
—GEORGE BERNARD SHAW

The creative life is propelled by a sense of purpose. What matters most to us directs the dance of doing and being. My friend Cynthia Kersey, founder of the Unstoppable Foundation, a visionary nonprofit organization that brings education and empowerment to children in developing countries, is a shining example of this. In my consulting work with the foundation, I was asked to help clarify and strengthen their brand, to identify a message that would be a powerful communicator of their mission. I applied the same techniques that are in this book to help them create their branding. As a filmmaker, I'm naturally inclined to go looking for the stories that speak to us at a deep level and learned of a young girl from Africa by the name of Susan.

The foundation had built an all-girls' high school in the Maasai Mara region of Kenya, and Susan's was the forty-first name on the waiting list. The problem was that the school had space for only forty students. When Susan received a message that she hadn't been accepted, she did what any unstoppable girl would do—she showed up at the school with the other forty girls and went directly to the administration office. Her dream was to become a doctor who could care for her neighbors in the remote village where she lived.

The principal said. "Susan, I'm sorry, but we only have room for forty girls." Susan left the office in tears. When the other students saw her crying, they huddled together to see what they could do. They knew that without an education, she had a bleak future ahead of her. After a few minutes, the girls approached the principal.

"Please don't make her go away. We will make room for her. We'll move our beds together. We'll share our books, pencils, and desks. Just let her stay!" Moved by the compassion of her students, the principal had a change of heart, and Susan became the forty-first girl. Her act of courage and vulnerability would eventually ripple outward, reaching people around the world.

Susan's story tells the tale of possibilities and miracles that the Unstoppable Foundation brings about more effectively than any logo or tagline ever could. It has worked well for the foundation as a branding story, and it has also been a powerful experience for me. It lifted me from a sense of creative accomplishment to one of creative achievement.

All creative acts are born of a desire to make change. We can make change on the surface of things, rearranging the furniture, or we can build an entirely new house. Creative accomplishment refers to an end result: *I made the movie. I knit the sweater. I baked the cake. I built the business.* But creative achievement goes beyond that to affect others. Collaborating with Cynthia, my personal creativity became a kind of "world creativity." I was able to have an impact on other people that changed me, too.

## VALUES—YOUR PERSONAL BEACONS OF LIGHT

As Cynthia's work demonstrates, creators are moved by the desire to improve the world in some way. Whether we go about it from a board-room, a laptop at our kitchen counter, or in the way we care for the people we love, that desire expresses our values.

In this chapter, you will focus your attention on the seven areas of creative life that you need to keep in balance. You will examine what matters to you, what guides you from inside. Each area is important on its own and important in how it affects the whole of your life. As we begin to pull on the threads in any one of these areas, all of them will respond. As you assess the current state of all seven areas, you can celebrate where you are already thriving and acknowledge where you might be experiencing limitation or dissatisfaction.

You rise above your conditioning by making commitments to feed, tend to, and engage with the values that are important to you. Clarity about where you are in and out of balance helps you to take action in beneficial ways.

# The Life Wheel

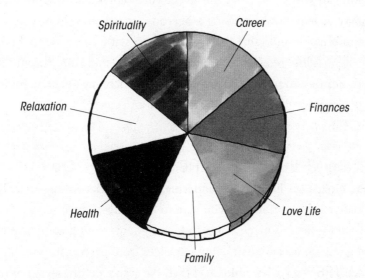

The life wheel is your values map, a tool for helping identify your priorities, goals, desires, dreams, and visions in career, finances, love life, family, health, relaxation, and spirituality. The life wheel is also a treasure map that can lead you to creative capacities that are waiting to be discovered. The life wheel above shows the seven areas of life in balance in equal measure.

## TAILORING THE LIFE WHEEL

Each one of us is living a life shaped by our values. Since our values and priorities shift at different times in our lives, we may need to adjust the life wheel occasionally. You can tailor sections to reflect your one-of-a-kind life. For example, if you are a stay-at-home parent, unemployed, or retired, you can consider altering the "career" section to focus on "creative expression," "creative work," or something along those lines. At any stage of your adult life, the career arena has to do with the *expression* of your life's purpose—although for many people today, work and business are *the* primary channels of creative expression. Work is one of our greatest art forms. It is also the backdrop against which we explore many life lessons.

You can also tailor "love life" to fit your individual circumstances. You may or may not be seeking a one-on-one partnership or you may be happily single and value the love you share with a dear friend. In this section, "love life" refers to your most intimate relationship. The guiding question to ask yourself is, "With whom do I share my deepest connection of closeness, tenderness, vulnerability, and trust?"

## RECONNECTING TO THE WHOLE OF YOUR LIFE

As you look at the life wheel, pondering each area, become aware of the proportion of attention that you give to each slice, which reflects how much you value it. Once upon a time, we got away with compartmentalizing our values and distracting ourselves from parts that were out of balance. Now we are less able to do that. We aren't "getting away with it" so well anymore. A values shortfall in one area will eventually show up elsewhere, and, in time, across the board. The good news is that tending to any one area that requires attention feeds creative energy to the whole wheel.

Paradoxically, the best way to tend to the whole of your life is to start with a single area that needs attention. When you fix one thing, everything changes.

Go through the following steps to assess your life wheel. I recommend tackling the easiest areas first. The more challenging areas quickly become easier to work with when you have created some positive momentum.

## Your Life Wheel—Taking Stock

**STEP 1**: Scoring the seven areas on a scale from 1 to 10. On a scale from 1 to 10, assign a number to each of the seven areas that represents your level of fulfillment and satisfaction. The number 1 represents being very dissatisfied or out of balance, the number 10 represents being very satisfied and fulfilled, and the numbers in between represent the various levels of limitation or flow you may be experiencing. For instance, you can trust your intuition to tell you if your finances are a 4 (perhaps savings have dwindled and income has temporarily decreased), a 7 (you have a consistent flow of financial inflow and outflow and feel basically secure), or another number that feels accurate to you.

Career: _____

Finances: _____

Love life: _____

Family: _____

Health: _____

Relaxation: _____

Spirituality: _____

**STEP 2**: Values. What do you most value in each area of your life? What experiences and activities do you value? What are the qualities of being and doing that you value? What are the resources and opportunities that you value? Who are the people you value? . . . etc.

Career:

_____

_____

_____

*Examples: The feeling of accomplishment; the satisfaction and joy of making a contribution; being a part of a team that has a shared mission; having the opportunity to use my gifts of communication, leadership, technical abilities (etc.).*

Finances:

_____

_____

_____

*Examples: The ability to take care of my family; the feeling of safety and security that my finances provide; having the means to travel; having the resources to further my education and training; having the ability to give to organizations and causes that matter to me (etc.).*

Love life:

_____

_____

_____

*Examples: The depth of emotional intimacy I share with my spouse; the affection and tenderness I give and receive; the passion that continues to burn after thirty years together (etc.).*

Family:

_____

_____

_____

*Examples: The bond I share with my children; the feeling of belonging that is the bedrock of my life; the adventures we share on our vacations; the fun and laughter we share at family gatherings; knowing that I am loved (etc.).*

Health:

_____

_____

_____

*Examples: Having the energy and vitality to pursue my dreams; being able to run marathons; having access to healthful food; having access to cutting-edge research and health information; receiving bodywork; going to my favorite exercise classes twice a week; feeling gratitude for my body's ability to heal and regenerate (etc.).*

Relaxation:

_____

_____

_____

*Examples: Sitting on my deck in the sun; remembering to breathe no matter what's happening around me; taking naps; taking walks with my partner after dinner to decompress; having thirty minutes to myself each day (etc.).*

Spirituality:

_____

_____

_____

*Examples: Going on contemplative retreats; attending church services with my family; reading inspirational books; sitting under my favorite tree and sensing my connection to nature; writing in my journal about all that I'm grateful for in my life (etc.).*

**STEP 3**: Desires and goals. What are your desires in each of the seven areas? What would you like to create, change, manifest, heal, or transform? Another way to know your desires is to look at the measurable goals you would like to attain.

Career:

_____

_____

_____

*Examples: Get promoted to a management position within a year; transition out of my job and into my own business within eighteen months; create a stronger bond with my team; finish my master's degree; get my teaching credentials; write an e-book; upgrade my website (etc.).*

Finances:

_____

_____

_____

*Examples: Double my income within one year; hire a new accountant; open a special savings account for my travel-the-world fund; design a crowd-funding campaign for my project (etc.).*

Love life:

_____

_____

_____

*Examples: Go on a date with my spouse once a week; attend couple's counseling; sign up for an online dating service; heal the shame that prevents me from opening my heart; forgive myself and those who have hurt me; go dancing with my partner even though I haven't danced in twenty years (etc.).*

Family:

_____

_____

_____

*Examples: Commit to time together each week without cell phones, computers, or other digital devices; reduce the number of hours we watch TV so we can have more time to talk and connect; call my parents regularly; organize a family reunion; practice being more open and vulnerable with my siblings (etc.).*

Health:

_____

_____

_____

*Examples: Go to sleep by 10 p.m.; watch my diet; treat myself with kind-ness; hire a trainer; lose ten pounds within the next six months; deal with the anger I'm still carrying about my divorce (etc.).*

Relaxation:

_____

_____

_____

*Examples: Go to tai chi classes on Saturday mornings; resume my monthly acupuncture treatments; experiment with playing the classical music station on my daily commute instead of the news station—notice what impact that has on me (etc.).*

Spirituality:

_____

_____

_____

*Examples: Before getting out of bed each morning, spend ten minutes visual-izing a day of connection and love; sign up for the church retreat taking place next week; spend time twice a month at the beach where I feel the presence of God roll in on each wave (etc.).*

STEP 4: The area of least resistance. In which area of your life are you eager, ready, and willing to act on right away? What section of your life wheel are you *looking forward* to addressing? Remember, difficult areas become easier to confront as we experience positive outcomes in any area.

The easiest area to tackle: _____

The first momentum-building action to take:

_____

_____

_____

**STEP 5**: The one area most in need of attention. Are you neglecting certain areas of your life and feeling the impact of that neglect? Would you call yourself a workaholic? Has anxiety over money, status, or power reduced your quality of life? Are you carrying stress or do you worry about job performance or intimate relationships that are impinging upon your daily life? Is there a part of your life that feels particularly stagnant or where you are experiencing an acute crisis? You can refer to your scoring to help you decide. Where did you assign the lowest number? The key is to proceed with honesty.

The one area most in need: _____

The core issues or challenges:

_____

_____

_____

## MAKING COMMITMENTS— THE WAY TOWARD BALANCE

As you explore these areas and look at the numbers you assigned to each one, consider how tending to one area affects the others. For example, if you gave your career a 3 and the area of relaxation a 5, you might first put attention on relaxation—on adding more fun, recreation, and leisure to your life and bringing that number up to a 7 or an 8. An increase in relaxation and pleasure can bring a new perspective on how to approach a career challenge. You might be dealing with a problem in your business or at work that feels too difficult to tackle at this moment, but your outlook could be very different after a few days or weeks of having more fun—going for hikes, watching movies, getting a massage, making time for loved ones, etc.

A good question to ask yourself is this: "Where would it be easier for me to make a commitment and to act on that commitment at this time?" Where are you most likely to follow through? Is it giving more attention every week to spending quality time with your family? Or is it being attentive to your primary relationship? Maybe you are most likely to commit to daily walks around your neighborhood to improve your health and fitness.

Trust the interconnected nature of your life. Look at the tips of your fingers; they each seem to be distinct and separate from every other finger. But as you move your gaze down, looking from the tips of your fingers to the palms of your hands, you see they are all connected. In the same way, as you flow more attention to one part of the life wheel, an area where you might be having bigger challenges suddenly begins to benefit from the increase in creative energy. It may be happening below the waterline of your awareness, yet the more difficult areas will become simpler and more receptive to change.

## THE EXAMPLE OF KATHERINE

One workshop participant, Katherine, said the area she most wanted to add to creatively was her love life. She had felt stagnant for years in that department, and creating a relationship seemed both scary and impossible. I asked Katherine to look at other areas of her life where her challenges and goals were not as daunting and to identify ways that she could give more attention to those simpler areas or situations, trusting that in due course more creative energy would become available for generating a romantic relationship. She felt a great deal of relief in approaching her life wheel in this way, saying that it unlocked her creativity and opened her eyes to possibilities and solutions that had previously evaded her.

## SEEING NEW POSSIBILITIES

The following visioning exercise will help you to breathe new life into the area you have identified as most needing attention and care.

## Visioning Exercise

### PART I—Growing Awareness

STEP 1: Write two or three paragraphs expressing your feelings about the area of your life most needing attention or where you're experiencing a challenge or crisis. Include how you feel about creating what you want in this area. Notice if you are feeling angry, numb, helpless, fearful, or another emotion. Also, describe any accompanying physical sensations. Do you feel tightness, heat, or pain in your body when you focus on this area? And what is your mental state? Are you mentally scattered, agitated, or blank?

STEP 2: As you begin to have a sense of what is going on internally through your writing, realize that the feelings you identify (like helplessness or frustration or hope) are coming from various aspects of you—the myriad intelligences that we began to look at in Chapter 1. For example, there is your creator intelligence that wants to create something new, and there is an intelligence that holds all your past experiences in this part of your life. The inner intelligence that is attuned to the past may feel hurt, anxious, distrustful, or have a memory of disappointment in this area. In other words, take note of the connection between your feelings and where those feelings are sourced. Be loving with the aspects of yourself that you discover.

### PART II—Engaging Your Senses

STEP 3: With this next step, you will be awakening vision through your senses. This is an opportunity to engage closely and tenderly with your desired outcome through your senses of touch, taste, smell, hearing, and seeing. This is a practice for holding in your imagination a clear sense—*a felt sense*—of what you want to create.

Begin by *practicing* your inner senses—the touch, taste, smell, hearing, and sight that you can bring alive through your imagination. Imagine what it feels like to stroke the head of a small furry dog, what it feels like to plunge your hand into a bucket of ice, or what it feels like to put your fingers on the doorknob of your front door.

Then imagine what it feels like to touch your desired outcome. What does it feel like to touch the hand of your partner, to put your hand in the warm sand of your dream vacation, to hold the check for services rendered, or to feel the strong muscles in your legs from your new workout regimen?

Practice your senses of taste, smell, hearing, and seeing in the same way—imaginatively. Turn on your inner senses before applying them to that which you wish to create with this next writing activity.

***Touch:*** What is it like to touch your desired outcome?

_____

_____

***Taste:*** What is the taste of your desired outcome?

_____

_____

***Smell:*** What is the fragrance or smell of your desired outcome?

_____

_____

***Hearing:*** What is the sound of your desired outcome?

_____

_____

***Seeing:*** What does your desired outcome look like?

_____

_____

By assessing your life wheel as you have done here, you are already responding to the call of creativity beyond your current pattern. I encourage you to engage your imagination frequently in this way. Make it a discipline to feel, see, and sense intensely what you want in your life. Through your intention and attention, you are instructing your subconscious self where and how you want that energy expressed.

Creating change requires focus and commitment. As you continue this process, positive changes will happen. Some of these changes might be visible immediately, and some of them will take place in more subtle ways. As you move through the remaining chapters of this book, notice how each of the topics relates to your life wheel. You can return to this section anytime in order to reassess your values and goals and to creatively fine-tune your life.

# *Try This!*

## SHOW ME YOUR VALUES

### *Your Creative Tools*

Gather a stack of magazines, a pair of scissors, your journal or a blank piece of paper, and a pen.

### *The Setting*

Give yourself five to ten minutes for this exercise. Pour a cup of coffee or tea and pull up a chair. Take a slow, deep breath to center yourself, and begin.

### *Your Values in Pictures*

Randomly select an image that represents one of your underlying values. Cut out that image and then label it—identifying the value that it symbolizes. For example, one might find an image of President Abraham Lincoln to cut out and label it "dignity." The quality of dignity is the value that has been identified.

### *The Story of Your Value*

Write the story of the value you have selected. This story could be told in one sentence or one page. The important thing is to be as vulnerable with yourself as possible.

Trust where your eyes and hands are guided when choosing an image. Our creative impulses are always communicating with us, and this exercise trains us to listen without overthinking or second-guessing. When I act upon and make changes as a result of what I learn, my relationship with creativity itself steps up and evolves.

The symbols we are drawn to always push us to stretch, grow, and respond. Once I cut out a picture of a garden snail. I decided that this was a representation of the importance I place on taking things slowly and easily. As I wrote about the slow and easy snail, I realized how frequently I move like molasses and, therefore, miss significant opportunities related to my career, my relationships, and other important aspects of my life. It was a whisper for me to change.

Repeat this exercise as desired.

## CHAPTER 6
# *The Most Amazing Thing*

*Follow your bliss and the universe will open doors
for you where there were only walls.*
—JOSEPH CAMPBELL

Let's take a panoramic look back at what you have done so far. You began to explore the creative intelligence that is your birthright, that is based on your innate sensing, knowing, and being. You explored the foundation of creativity, when will and action give rise to imagining and feeling. You reconnected with your body, where thoughts and feelings release creative energy. You took inventory of your career, finances, love life, family, health, relaxation, and spirituality, opening wide the lens of perception in order to evaluate your current desires, needs, and values.

Now it is time to narrow your focus with laserlike precision.

## THE MOST AMAZING THING

I would like you to take a few moments to reflect on a time when you were in the flow. This is not a formal exercise, but a moment to daydream.

Take a few slow, deep breaths and recall a time when you felt inspired, open, and connected to yourself and those around you. It might be when you were falling in love, watching your children, drinking in a sunset, or making the perfect golf shot. Or it might be a time when you were putting Christmas gifts under the tree or delivering a presentation to a group of your colleagues, a time when you knew that you were making a contribution to others or to something greater than yourself.

When you have that recollection in mind, imagine it in present time, as if it is happening right now. What is the quality of that experience? What is the feeling of that experience? Whatever the quality or feeling is for you, think of it as an essential nutrient. A natural resource. A force of extraordinary power. This essential quality or feeling is what I call *The Most Amazing Thing*. The Most Amazing Thing is a switch that turns you on. Like a personal GPS, it broadcasts a signal that tells you when you're moving toward or away from what makes you truly alive. It carries a frequency that generates creative energies and passions. When you know what The Most Amazing Thing is for you, you can choose to act based on that knowing. You can decide where your energy goes. Any creative project, whether a work of art, a business endeavor, a health makeover, or a close relationship, can become an expression of The Most Amazing Thing. Attuning yourself to this quality or feeling is a way to align with your creative output and to direct it.

When you use your *life* to express what is most amazing to you, you are aligning yourself with powers of creativity beyond your current conceptions of what you know.

How is this so?

No matter how much planning and list making we do, the fact is that creativity is not born in the head. It's not even of this world. It is received as a gift from beyond, delivered as a rush or wave of inspiration. It is a love story—will and action merging with imagination, feeling, and being.

To be an intimate partner with creativity, put down your pen, paintbrush, or iPad for a moment and open your heart and mind to receiving those gifts and bringing them into the world to the best of your ability.

> *Creativity is a love story—will and action merging with imagination, feeling, and being.*

## ACCEPT NO SUBSTITUTES

We are often in hot pursuit of *substitutes* for The Most Amazing Thing. We think that we're after the job, the new account, the house, the partner, or the money. But those things alone are never The Most Amazing Thing. What we really want lies under those outward manifestations.

Beneath the desire for money can be a hunger for security, power, freedom, or love. Money is always a substitute for something deeper.

The precise quality or feeling that one is looking for through the pursuit of substitutes is unique and personal.

When I find myself desiring *anything*—a person, an object, a thing— I try to remember to ask, "What is it that is really attracting me? What is the *felt experience* below the surface of things that I am longing for?"

When I don't look below the surface at my true needs and desires, other agendas take over. Misdirected, I focus my energies into competing, manipulating, persuading, or attempting to control. I am not alone in this. It is what separates us from the wild joy of being vehicles for creative expression.

On the other hand, understanding The Most Amazing Thing can be a catalyst for moving past challenges and blockages. Maybe you don't feel like working, you have writer's block, or are awash in self-doubt. Connecting with The Most Amazing Thing cracks open the door again to inspiration and flow.

### Discovering the Most Amazing Thing—The Exercise

*The Event or Experience*

Think about an event, circumstance, or experience that gives you the most direct connection with your creative self. What puts you in the stream of your creative flow?

_____

_____

_____

### One Paragraph

Bring that event or experience into the present moment and ask yourself, "What is it about this that is so important to me? Why am I so moved? What do I find so inspiring? What are the feelings and the qualities of being that I associate with it?" *Remember, it is never the project, the goal, or the thing. It is the quality or feeling beneath the thing.*

Develop your thoughts into a paragraph.

_____

_____

_____

_____

_____

_____

_____

_____

_____

_____

### One Sentence

Distill the paragraph above into one sentence that describes the essential quality, feeling, or state.

_____

_____

### One Word/Phrase—The Most Amazing Thing

Go deeper. What is the one word or phrase that encapsulates the quality or feeling that is so valuable to you? Is it peace, tranquility, joy? Is it passion, courage, hopefulness? Know that it is going to be a qualitative experience, and look beyond the first thing that comes to mind. If a word such as *family* or *connection* comes to you, what is the feeling beneath that? Is it relief? Belonging? Being loved? If *respect* is the word that comes to you, what is the feeling that respect gives you?

Is it confidence? Go deeper still. Is it a feeling of value? Trust your intuition while plumbing the depths for your word or phrase. Trust your inner knowing.

_____

_____

## THE ULTIMATE PRACTICE—A LOVE AFFAIR WITH THE MOST AMAZING THING

The Most Amazing Thing that you have identified doesn't have to be the bottom line, the final word. You can play with this exercise as much as you want, and I encourage you to do that. Enjoy the process of discovery. Each time you practice this you are moving toward positive self-talk. You are retraining yourself. You are choosing where you are placing your focus, the path of creative mastery. At any time, you can ask yourself:

Am I focusing on The Most Amazing Thing, or am I focusing on a substitute?

Am I choosing where my attention and energy are going, or are they up for grabs?

Practice thinking about and feeling The Most Amazing Thing. Practice in the car, in the elevator, waiting for your computer to warm up. It will become second nature.

I practice all day. Sure, I still have plenty of negative self-talk that comes up, but more and more I am attuned to The Most Amazing Thing.

There is no right or wrong to this. Creators decide where to focus their energy and what to give their attention to. Energy follows attention, so practice, practice, practice.

*Energy follows attention, so practice, practice, practice.*

I once worked with a corporate executive whom I'll call Ellen. Ellen was doing well in her career but had reached a point where she was merely going through the motions. She was discouraged because she felt creatively blocked and unfulfilled, and the outward indicators of success were giving her minimal satisfaction. Together, we focused on the feeling she was looking for, that she was *longing* for. Ellen realized that what she craved was the experience of a freedom of movement; an unfettered, joyful *freedom*. This freedom was The Most Amazing Thing for her, and it became a beacon, lighting the way back to her true essence. Beneath the overlay of structured thinking, feeling, and imagining is our real self, and Ellen turned toward hers with giddy abandon. Now she is a virtuoso at noticing the subtlest experiences that spark her sense of freedom. She has an awareness of flow in her life, and her work is no longer a drudge. She now offers workshops for women who feel like she used to feel—women who want to rediscover their passion beyond their roles as mothers, wives, and businesswomen.

Recently, I received a call from a studio executive whom I've known for many years. The Most Amazing Thing for him was the feeling of waking up to new possibilities. He had embarked on a spiritual quest involving meditation and was beginning a postretirement career as a coach to support other men and women wanting to break out of conditioned roles.

Both of these people discovered that The Most Amazing Thing isn't a thought alone. And it's not a thing. It is an experience in the body. Though you may sometimes overlook these doorways of aliveness, what makes them amazing is that they have the power to re-create your life.

# CHAPTER 7

## *The Four Anesthetics*

*When things are shaky and nothing is working,*
*we might realize that we are on the verge of something.*
—PEMA CHÖDRÖN

Right now, you might be looking for the next line of dialogue for your screenplay, or working on the design and flow of a slide presentation that you'll deliver to coworkers next week. Maybe you are searching for a creative new way to communicate with your teenager, one that will restore a feeling of connection between the two of you.

When you think of your task, do you feel clear and inspired? Or do you feel muddled, perhaps even stopped in your tracks?

Hitting a creative wall happens to everyone. However frustrating or disheartening this might be, what can seem like a creative impasse is an opportunity for greater self-understanding and freedom.

One of the fundamental reasons we run into roadblocks is because we have maxed out the creative possibilities of our existing brain patterning. Within the confines of our creative conditioning—the structured imagining that we have adopted from other people's thinking, feeling, beliefs, and values—we continue to refer to the same mental maps when approaching our projects and plans. While we may be called toward innovation, we find ourselves stuck—thinking the same thoughts, feeling the same feelings, and getting nowhere fast.

Are your thinking and feeling creating the outcomes you want? Is the internal dialogue that mirrors your thoughts and feelings, your self-talk, enhancing creative flow or impeding it? What are you saying to yourself? Are you encouraging yourself or telling yourself stories of limitation and frustration?

> *What can seem like a creative impasse is an opportunity for greater self-understanding and freedom.*

## THE IMPACT OF OUR INNER DIALOGUE

My friend Master Chunyi Lin, founder and creator of Spring Forest Qigong, showed me a dramatic exercise that demonstrates the impact of thinking and feeling on our body, mind, and spirit.

## Finger-Growing Game

STEP 1: Find the lines at the bottom of the palms of your hands where your wrist begins. Most of us have either two or three pronounced lines there. Put these two or three lines together, matching or aligning them. Then put your palms together.

STEP 2: Compare the lengths of your fingers. Most of us have fingers that are slightly longer on one hand than the other.

STEP 3: Raise the hand with the shorter fingers and put the hand with the longer fingers down, laying it gently on your lower stomach. Slightly stretch open the hand that is raised, and with a smile on your face, gently close your eyes.

STEP 4: While your hands are in this position, repeat in your mind, "My fingers are growing longer, longer, longer, longer; they are growing longer, longer, longer, and still longer."

Repeat this to yourself with complete confidence for a few seconds, *knowing* that the fingers on your raised hand are growing longer.

**STEP 5**: Open your eyes and compare your hands again in the same way, matching up the lines on your wrists and putting your palms together.

Your shorter fingers became longer, didn't they? Isn't that wild!?

**STEP 6**: Put your fingers back to normal. Open your hands and say to yourself, "My fingers come back to normal." You only need to say that once. Line up your palms at the wrist again and compare your fingers now. Back to usual, right?

This is just a small taste of how you are directing yourself. With this powerful experience in mind, imagine the effects of negative self-talk on your creative life. Are your thoughts, perceptions, and feelings supporting new growth and possibility?

For you to innovate or create something new, you must destroy something old. You have to dismantle repetitive emotional habits that activate negative thoughts and feelings so that you can conceive and perceive invention.

## THE FOUR ANESTHETICS

Like a deer in the headlights, we become inwardly immobilized when we are distressed or overwhelmed. Some thoughts and feelings, when mixed together, are particularly potent anesthetics. These are substitute feelings that we turn to in order to numb more powerful emotions, both positive and negative, that we are afraid of. We learn how to use these numbing agents at a very early age; they help us handle any feelings that are too much for us.

When I was very little, my mom and dad were out one evening, and I began to worry that they would never come back. That fear of abandonment, of being left alone or left with strangers, was an emotion that I was unequipped to handle. Instead I imagined something else, something I could manage. I created this story:

"If only I had been better behaved."

"If only I had been good."
"If only I had been nicer than I was."
"I should have been different."

It is the "shoulda, coulda, woulda" dilemma. These were tough emotions for a child, but they were emotions I could deal with. Like all anesthetics, they numbed me from feeling the more intense emotions of despair, panic, and the terror of abandonment.

As an adult, I am now able to handle all the feelings I figured out how to avoid as a child. I am able to, but I don't necessarily. Defaulting to the anesthetics is still an easy way out. But the price of numbing with anesthetics is my raw creative energy.

That's a bad bargain.

The four emotional anesthetics are especially effective at shutting down creativity:

- self-pity
- blame
- guilt
- control

These four states will undermine flow, always. Period.

Just as choices, thoughts, and beliefs are hardwired in the brain, the four anesthetics can become hardwired, but with practice and commitment, you can recognize and break free of them. If you take only one thing from this book, an awareness of the four anesthetics should be it.

Understand this, and you will thrive—creatively and emotionally.

## Recognizing the Anesthetics—The Exercise

STEP 1—The desire: Become aware of something you want to create, or something you already have and want to maintain. Perhaps you desire a relationship or you want to maintain the loving relationship that you already have. Do you desire satisfying work, sound health, or financial stability? What is your strongest desire at this time?

_____

_____

**STEP 2—The fear:** Become aware of any fear that may be connected to creating or maintaining the object of your desire. For example, it could be a fear of not being good enough to attract or create what you want. Or it could be a fear of losing someone dear to you, or the loss of financial stability. The more we value something, the more we fear its potential loss. Do you have a fear of losing your career, reputation, health, or love? Imagine the threat, and write the story that your fear has to tell about it.

_____

_____

_____

_____

_____

_____

**STEP 3—The road of thoughts and feelings:** Close your eyes and take three slow, deep breaths to relax. Imagine yourself walking down a road toward your feared outcome. Walk slowly and deliberately, sensing the thoughts and feelings that arise as you approach your fear. You don't need to specifically identify each one. Putting one foot in front of the other, be aware of each interruption taking you off course onto a dangerous soft shoulder. Return your attention to your feared outcome, and get back on the road.

Use the following questions to recognize how the four anesthetics may be numbing the powerful emotions of your dreaded scenario.

*Is self-pity tied in with my feared outcome? Is my ability to imagine a positive outcome obscured by a belief that I am a victim in this area of life?*

*Is feeling sorry for myself overriding my desire? If so, you've identified an anesthetic.*

*Am I blaming myself or someone else for feeling undeserving, inadequate, or fearful? Am I blaming past or current circumstances for why I can't have what I want, or why I think I will lose what I have? If so, recognize it's an anesthetic.*

*Is my fear covering up guilt that I have about an experience from my past or present? If so, real feelings are trapped underneath, as well as raw creative energy.*

*When I look beneath my fear, do I find an urge to control a situation, a relationship, or a person? Am I looking for a guaranteed outcome? If so, anesthetic.*

**STEP 4—Recognize and acknowledge:** Keep walking the road to your feared outcome. Your mission is to recognize and acknowledge what is there—real or anesthetic? Notice and keep moving.

**STEP 5—Real emotions:** Choose to experience your real emotions and release the anesthetics. Intensely feel your real emotions; they will change and dissipate. As you continue to move through your feared outcome, feeling only your real emotions, you will start to experience the powerful feelings of creativity and flow that lie underneath.

In a stream-of-consciousness manner, describe feeling your real emotions and how they are experienced in your body.

_____

_____

_____

_____

_____

_____

_____

_____

_____

Anesthetics are inventions of the mind that numb us from feeling real emotions that caused us discomfort in the past. Ironically, the anesthetics are almost always more painful than the feelings they are numbing. Unlike anesthetics, real emotions always dissipate when felt. Like dinner guests, who may be either difficult or delightful, real emotions eventually leave. Therein lies the creative breakthrough. Feeling your real emotions always opens you up to something new.

## THE CREATIVE POWER OF
## INTENTION AND ATTENTION

"If you build it, they will come."

The movie *Field of Dreams* gave us one of the most powerful, true statements about the creative process. It acknowledges that intention combined with attention and follow-through is critical to all creative acts, whether we are talking about creating specific works of art or how creation itself works.

Our energy follows our attention, always.

Our attention is less likely to be hijacked by emotional anesthetics and habituated thought patterns as we learn to direct it. As we make a practice of noticing where our attention is going, we can more easily see the intentions underlying our actions, thus becoming more responsible for the choices we make.

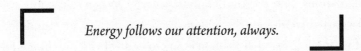

*Energy follows our attention, always.*

At a glance, the energetic ecosystem we are exploring here looks like this:

- intention
- attention
- energy

- responsibility
- choice
- follow-through

When we work with these faculties consciously, we are harnessing a massive amount of creative power. I had a crash course in this from a man named Wyatt Webb. At first meeting, Wyatt strikes you as a real cowboy, a salt-of-the-earth kind of guy, grizzled, with white hair under a big dusty hat. His wise direction awakened me from certain feeling patterns that had become anesthetics for me.

Wyatt works with horses, and he had one waiting for me early one morning. He gave me clear instructions, "You're going to clean the muck out from the horse's shoe, Barnet. When you step up to the horse, you'll grab her firmly, just on the tendon above the hoof, and she will lift her foot."

I bent down to grab the horse's hoof, but I couldn't budge it. That hoof might as well have been planted in cement. It wasn't going anywhere. Then I started petting the horse.

Wyatt said, "Do you always reward failure?"

I thought about that for a second. My stomach turned.

Wyatt probed a little deeper. "What are you *doing* there?"

"Well, I was trying to make a friend of the horse. I was just trying to be known by her."

Very patiently, Wyatt said, "This animal does not respond to your manipulations. She responds only to energy. When you come to her with a particular energy, she will respond. But if you come muddied up by other intentions, such as 'I am going to control you into liking me so you will lift your foot,' forget it. *When you come clearly with one intention, she will immediately respond.*"

That floored me.

"How often do you conduct yourself like this?" continued Wyatt. "In what other areas do you get so flustered? How much do you try to control life?"

Suddenly I understood that my ability to connect, to interact, *to create* was being influenced by habituated internal forces—such as trying to manipulate. If I make friends with this horse, she will like me, she will accommodate me. I realized how much I have done this in my life. I understood it with such perfect clarity that right there I knew I could drop it. I could drop my ulterior motives. And I did.

Wyatt told me to try again. I walked up to the horse with just the intent to lift her leg and that leg flew up the instant I touched it. It was an amazing moment of "show-and-tell." The natural world is not responsive to controlling manipulations. When I approached the horse with clarified intention, her leg flew up.

Every step we take toward letting go of anesthetizing behaviors opens us to more creative flow.

## DEVELOPING CREATIVE PLASTICITY

The brain's ability to reconfigure itself by forming new neural connections and synapses at any stage of life is called *neuroplasticity*. Until recently, scientists believed that we are born with a set of unchanging biological blueprints that dictate that we inevitably lose our faculties through illness, toxicity, trauma, stress, and aging. However, new findings show that neuroplasticity allows brain cells to compensate for disease and injury and create new pathways that can help us heal or reclaim our functions.

Similarly, the principles and activities in this book are designed to bring about what I call *creative plasticity*, an imaginative malleability that can serve you in a multitude of ways—from sourcing a new idea to resolving acute or chronic problems. To create self-reinforcing neural patterns, intention and attention are keys to this fluidity. That is why practice—*which is focused expression of intention and attention*—is so important. It establishes new neural patterns that welcome and enhance creative flow.

We will put this to the test with the following four exercises.

## REWIRING THE BRAIN THROUGH RELAXATION

When we are relaxed, we are much more likely to have those big "Aha" creative breakthrough moments, those flashes of insight when the solution to a seemingly impossible problem reveals itself. Relaxation enables us to go inward, to make connections that might go unrecognized when we are mentally distracted or experiencing stress. Alpha brain waves occur when we are relaxed and calm. This slower frequency of brain activity, occurring between eight to twelve cycles per second, correlates with a state of receptivity. Characteristic of wakeful rest, alpha brain waves provide a bridge between the conscious mind and the subconscious mind, paving the way for creativity. Walking in nature, listening to soothing music, or meditating are some ways that we can promote this relaxation response in the brain, which results in a heightened ability to concentrate, focus, learn, visualize, and imagine.

The following breathing exercise will quickly put you in touch with your alpha brain waves, encouraging a state of relaxation. As a simple method for rewiring the neural patterns in your brain, you can use it to start your day or kick-start a creative work session. You will find it especially effective when you're feeling overwhelmed or unclear.

### Mindful Breathing Technique

Set a timer so you don't have to think about time elapsed or look at a clock.

For two to three minutes, settle into a comfortable position in your chair, close your eyes, and breathe through the nose.

Bring your full attention to the experience of the breath entering and then leaving your nose.

If you become distracted by a thought or drift off, gently bring your attention back to the focus on your breath entering and leaving your nose.

When you are ready, come back to center, and slowly open your eyes.

In addition to mindful breathing, here are a few of my favorite ways to incorporate activities that promote alpha brain waves:

- Step away from your desk or get out of the office.
- Take a nap.
- Daydream.
- Take a long, warm shower.
- Sit by a body of water—river, stream, lake, pond, or sea.
- Go for a walk in nature.

## INTERRUPTING HABITUATED PATTERNS OF THOUGHT AND FEELING

You have far more control over your physical, emotional, and mental states than you realize. Within seconds, you can use the power of conscious breathing and imagination to change your state of being—to release stress and reconnect with yourself and the world around you.

The following practice, which you can use anytime and in any place, is ideal for creating an intention to be more open and receptive, shifting out of a negative mood, preparing for a presentation or meeting, getting ready for a date with your partner, recalibrating your senses for a productive work session, etc. Use it whenever you want to meet the moment with your full presence.

### Stopping the Function of Your Reality

Take three slow, deep breaths to relax.

Imagine that you are slowing *everything* down. Imagine that you are slowing down your brain waves. Slowing down your blood flow. Slowing down your heartbeat. Slowing down the world.

Now, imagine that everything has come to a stop. Your brain waves. Your blood flow. Your heartbeat. Your breathing. Everything has come to a gentle stop.

Rest in the stillness.

After about a minute, slowly come back to your normal pace and rhythm.

Refreshed, you will be ready to go about your business . . . more relaxed, open, and creatively receptive.

## REARRANGING THE ROUTINE OF YOUR LIFE

Doing ordinary things in a different order, consciously mixing things up, rewires and refires the flow of creativity. Try different approaches to routine activities:

- Sleep on a different side of the bed.
- Drink from a cup instead of a glass.
- Use chopsticks instead of a fork.
- Follow a new path through the grocery store.
- Find new routes for your drive or walk to work.
- Fold the laundry in a different room.
- Greet people in a new way.
- Answer your phone in new ways.
- Reposition the items on your desk.

By rearranging routines, you actively generate new perspectives. Creativity does not come unbidden. You have to encounter it and invite it. Ask yourself, "How can I approach common things more inventively?" Have fun with it. Like the woman I saw peel a banana from the bottom up!

## RESOLVING ACUTE OR CHRONIC PROBLEMS

Do you have a challenge in any part of your life that is asking you for an attention/intention intervention? Consider a social scenario that bothers you. Maybe one of your coworkers talks to you so much that you can't get your work done, your neighbor complains about your dog barking, or your child throws tantrums when you are doing homework together. Once you have the problem in mind, you are ready for the following exercise.

## The Stream-of-Consciousness Solution

**Setting the stage:** This creative practice is an opportunity to direct your attention toward a problem-solving task without being distracted by perfectionism, judgments of others, self-judgments, or limiting thoughts and feelings. It is also a chance to suspend judgment on the quality of your solutions.

Set your timer for three minutes. Then take a few centering breaths.

**STEP 1**: Write your problematic scenario at the top of your page in a few words.

**STEP 2**: Write down as many ways to solve this problem as you can think of. Write without judging the quality of your solutions. (*This practice of nonjudgment is a major asset for the creative life.*)

**STEP 3**: When you feel complete, review your list. Are there any surprises? Like panning for gold, sift out the ideas that don't resonate strongly and hold on to the gems—the solutions that excite you.

**STEP 4**: Sifting further, choose one that sparkles the most. If there are any action steps involved with your solution, write down the specifics— clarify the when, where, and how.

## THE GIFT OF DAILY PRACTICE

To reach and stretch in new directions, engage in activities and rituals that awaken positive potentials. Practice, because your old linear, logical approaches, as valuable as they are, are not valuable *enough*, not extensive *enough*. Engage in practices that stir the imagination, that stir deeper realms of thought and feeling. Challenge yourself to push in the clutch on old brain patternings and make the shift toward something brand new. Fire up virgin connections.

With practice, you begin to forge entirely new maps that take you out of the ruts of structured imaging.

To see bigger and faster results, make a commitment to practice on a daily basis. You will be amazed at the results. From your love life, to career, to finances, to health, and beyond, you will be generating new neural networks that will enrich and widen your world.

## CHAPTER 8
# *The Faces of Obstruction*

*Nature loves courage. You make the commitment and nature
will respond to that commitment by removing impossible obstacles.*
—TERENCE MCKENNA

In the Chinese language, the word for *crisis* shares a character with the word for *opportunity*. This is a symbolic reminder to go looking for the light switch when we find ourselves in the dark, when we are going through a challenging period or feel lost. Sometimes we can find ourselves creatively "lost"—filled with self-doubt, uninspired, or otherwise blocked. However, the blockages we can encounter when we want to create something new give us an opportunity to discover a great deal about ourselves. The creative walls we run into give us the opportunity to discover what is operating below the surface of our awareness.

## SURFACING SUBTEXT

Key to the well-trodden mental maps and emotional anesthetics we have explored are the internal scripts that run much of the time. In the story line of our day-to-day lives, this is known as subtext. Setting a particular mood and direction, subtext holds all the elements that give rise to our strategies for responding to life and living life—our history, beliefs, and the conditioning that shapes our structured imagining. And while subtext always includes our intentions, it is much more than intention alone.

To an actor or director, *subtext* is a word for all the unspoken thoughts, feelings, and motivations a performer brings to her role. Subtext is always unspoken, yet it is the most eloquent aspect of an actor's performance, coloring every speech and action. But subtext is not to be found in the script. It comes from the actor's unique interpretation of the story, mined from personal memory, life experience, and imagination.

Imagine you're watching an on-screen drama. In it, a businessperson calls her fiancé from her hotel room out of town.

"I miss you," she says.

Does she say it with her full attention or with one eye on cable news? Is she thinking about a potential client she saw in the bar? Is she seductive, sleepy, or rushing him off the line? The same words can be mouthed from infinite frames of mind. The subtext always expresses our deeper motivations, the under-the-table and subconscious agendas that truly run our lives, including how we approach our creative expression. This is the level of communication we sense when we are "reading between the lines."

Just as characters in the movies know very little about the underlying outlooks that drive them, we don't generally start out aware of the power of our own subtexts in the various parts of our lives. Sometimes we need to turn to methods of personal growth or spirituality in order to figure out our subtexts. All communication begins at the level of the subconscious and all communication benefits from self-awareness. The more we realize this, the more powerfully we can apply that knowledge to the creation of everything—from art, to business, to life.

The deepest creativity happens in the subtext. This is the reason why Shakespeare can be performed in theaters around the globe and still remain fresh. Even though the text is the same, the production is always different. The responsibility of a director, the *decider*, is to choose the subtext. Just as the director chooses the subtext of a play or a film, we choose our own subtexts, as well. We are always creating. Whenever we supply the subtext to our experience, we are creating.

An exercise I include in some of my workshops reveals the deeper nature of subtext and demonstrates that stories do not live in the facts or the plot. The meaning behind our stories, which is always personal, only exists in the invisible threads that bind them together.

In this exercise, we are going to perform what in the movie business is called a script analysis. Actors and directors routinely do this. Imagine a photograph of a young boy seated in a chair underneath a bridge. What are the facts of the scene?

The boy is wearing shorts.

He has long hair and glasses.

He is facing in the direction of somebody who is walking away.

The person walking away appears to be a man.

The man is wearing a suit.

You might say something like, "It's a sad boy sitting on a chair." Or, "He's hungry and alone." Are those facts? All we know is that there is a boy sitting on a chair. Can we even say how old he is? We can only say that he appears to be a young boy.

Continuing on, we discover more facts.

It's daylight.

There is a large suspension bridge above him.

There are cars on the bridge.

It might be the Bay Bridge from San Francisco to Oakland, but we can't know that for certain. We can only know that there is a boy sitting under a suspension bridge.

Finally, I would ask you to take five minutes to write a short story, weaving together the facts that we analyzed with what you think might be going on. You might come up with something like this: "The boy is waiting because his father ran out of gas and is going for help. The boy has been abandoned and is now homeless. The bridge represents the joining of two different worldviews—those of the child and the adult."

Whether we ask ten people or a hundred, we would quickly discover that every story is totally different. Some might be about loss, some about mystery. But they are never remotely the same. The reason is, we don't see the world the way *it* is. We see it the way *we* are.

Even though the facts of your life may be shared with the people around you, YOU make the difference. You add the emotional complexity, the meaning, the subtext. You are the creator. And although you and I might agree that the sky is blue and the grass is green, when we scratch beneath the details with an exercise like this one, we can see that we are each having a singular experience.

I once used script analysis with a learning company that wanted to fine-tune their mission statement and company identity. During the exercise, it became apparent that everyone in the room had entirely different stories attached to a presumed straightforward mission statement. They realized they could not take for granted that their priorities and values were being communicated, so they began to fill in clarifying details for each other. As they contributed their ideas, thoughts, and feelings with greater specificity, a powerful new identity emerged, and they became more effective in their offerings.

Whenever unexamined outlooks come to the surface, surprising things can happen. Sometimes it can be challenging, as it was for an executive of a tech company who wanted to expand her team's capacity for innovation. The script analysis exercise took the lid off differing points of view and many unspoken assumptions came to light. After the executive shared with everyone what had come up for her during the exercise, she quickly retreated, angry about feeling exposed and vulnerable in front of the group. Creative leadership always requires strength of vulnerability, including the willingness to recognize and admit to personal or group dynamics that are blocking forward momentum. Vulnerability is essential for establishing an environment where change is encouraged and creativity is allowed to flourish.

Another time I worked with a client who managed promotions and publicity for a group of elite spas and hotels. She experienced similar challenges as the tech executive, but the obstructions were surfacing with her business partner rather than with a team. The script analysis exercise helped untangle wires that had gotten crossed related to their communication, points of view, and operating styles. It helped her recognize a tendency toward rigid thinking and snap judgments that she had adopted earlier in life as a way to create a sense of personal power. They were isolating her in her partnership. Script analysis gave my client greater empathy for both herself and her partner. She became more responsive and less reactive. In a short amount of time, they were working together more effectively and their business prospered.

> *Creative leadership always requires*
> *strength of vulnerability.*

Without the ability to discover and change our personal beliefs, feelings, and conditioned thinking, we repeat and respond to every experience life has to offer through the same filters and patterns. Nothing ever changes. But recognizing and breaking patterns of inflexibility allow creativity to emerge and surge. Even small changes in subtext can create major changes in our life stories. One of the greatest gifts of a creative life is the power to become aware of subtext. Here is a simple awareness practice:

- Pay attention to your thoughts and feelings, especially in times of stress.
- Ask yourself, "Where am I coming from?"
- Repeat this question over and over for every answer you get, until you sense a bottom line. That is subtext.

Surfacing subtext in this way signals a willingness to grow and change. And this is precisely when we want to increase our awareness of the obstructions that might surface as well.

## OBSTRUCTIONS TO CHANGE

When we have a desire to begin something new, we are most likely to encounter impediments to change. Obstruction has two common behavioral traits to be aware of:

- Obstruction often comes up in opposition to the things that we most want to create and most want to do.
- Obstruction tends to occur when we are taking *big* steps forward, evolving to the next greatest expression of ourselves.

## WHAT IS OBSTRUCTION?

According to the *Oxford American Dictionary*, obstruction is "a thing that impedes or prevents passage or progress; an obstacle or blockage." In other words, it's the enemy of creativity. With the stress that it generates, obstruction is a massive energy drain that can temporarily leave us unable to receive inspiration or to notice opportunity when it arrives. The best way to illustrate this is to put a spotlight on the habituated behaviors, mental states, and internal scripts that are obstruction's favorite forms of expression whether operating alone or in intricate combinations.

- **Perfectionism**—having to "do it right," usually carried through from childhood when we learned to look for outside validation and compare and contrast ourselves with others
- **Procrastination**—checking email, Facebook, and other distractions; visiting the refrigerator; watching TV, texting, or making phone calls rather than tending to the creative process
- **Losing focus**—getting sleepy or otherwise having a hard time concentrating (a cousin of procrastination)
- **Feeling overwhelmed**—taking on too much
- **Boredom or retreat**—not taking on enough
- **Drama**—looking for/getting involved in family blowups, misunderstandings at work, financial chaos, martyred behavior, and other persistent troubles

- **Judgment-making**—dispensing black-and-white pronouncements about oneself or others that cut off connection and put a metaphorical wall between us and creative possibility
- **Fear**—avoiding/stopping due to fear of failure, self-doubt, and humiliation
- **Anger**—feeling alienated/apathetic/tired/depressed due to anger that is unexpressed and unresolved

The voice of obstruction can sound like this:
- "I don't have what it takes to get this done."
- "Who am I to do this? I'm way out of my league."
- "I don't have the right connections."
- "I don't have the proper training or education."
- "Someone else can do it better than I can."
- "Someone else has already done it."
- "Does the world really need another _____ (*start-up, album, book, play, restaurant, documentary, etc.*)?"

## WHEN OBSTRUCTION BECOMES SELF-SABOTAGE

These forces of obstruction bottle up creativity. With enough repetition, an obstruction easily turns into full-blown self-sabotage. If we are embroiled in relationship drama, there is little (if any) time, energy, or space for creativity to happen. Nothing creative gets done. When procrastination becomes a chronic behavior rather than a momentary diversion, creativity gets lost in trivialities. Both are powerful kinds of sabotage.

Years ago, I was working on a film and found myself face-to-face with my own saboteur. Grappling with self-doubt and perfectionism, I was overwhelmed with thoughts such as, "I'm *way* out of my league here." Feeling insecure, I responded to many decisions and requests with an automatic *no*. It was the fastest way to feel in control of my outer circumstances when I felt anything but confident inside myself. My self-sabotaging behavior caused dissension and conflict with my collaborators, and I almost got fired. The final movie wasn't what it could have been, nor was the experience of making it.

When obstructions are indulged and unacknowledged, they become sabotaging. They hurt you. And they hurt the people around you. But don't despair if you recognize yourself engaged in this kind of behavior. The saboteur is always a reaction to insecurity and perfectionism. We don't have to do it perfectly. Recognize the obstruction, admit it, and summon the courage to change.

We are trained to aspire to "doing it right." As children, we don't start out looking to see whether we're doing it right. We exist in the moment, expressing ourselves. Gradually, after the eighth or fiftieth person says, "That's great. What you did is really wonderful," we become more interested in the validation than in experiencing the creativity that is flowing through us. Ever so slowly, we learn to compare, contrast, and compete. When the validation doesn't come the next time, we wonder what we did wrong. That is when creativity is no longer about self-expression; it is about manipulating for an outside response.

## Recognizing and Acknowledging Obstruction—
## A Timed-Writing Exercise

STEP 1: Set a timer for five minutes.

STEP 2: Without lifting your pen and without stopping, write down all the ways that you "do" obstruction. Take a slow, deep breath to connect with yourself—and then begin.

If you run out of something to say before the five minutes are up: Keep writing! Restart with this sentence: *"I'm so obstructed that I've run out of things to say, and I would really love to stop writing but I'm not going to stop because I made a commitment to exploring my obstruction."* You can rewrite this sentence until new words flow from your pen.

Now it is time to dialogue with your obstruction. Finding out what it has to tell you will free up your reservoir of creative energy.

## The Bottom Line of Your Obstruction— A Writing Exercise

**STEP 1**: Imagine that you are sitting down to be creative. You are at your desk, drawing table, easel, keyboard, countertop, or in your favorite chair. There is something you want to create—a goal to attain, a dream to fulfill, or a contribution to make—and you feel stress building in anticipation of this creative work.

**STEP 2**: Name or describe the stressful thoughts, feelings, and sensations that come up in relationship to this creativity session. Without censoring yourself, write them all down.

**STEP 3**: Choose the thought, feeling, or sensation that feels most stressful and let it speak to you. When you feel that stress come up, ask it the following question: "Where am I coming from?" Then repeat that question for every answer you get until you sense that you have come to a bottom line.

**EXAMPLE**: "I'm feeling really tired. I was going to paint (*or sit down at the piano or plant seeds in the garden or spend quality time with my partner*), but I'm totally exhausted."
*Question:* "Where am I coming from?"
*Answer:* "I really don't want to put in any effort or to work today."
*Question:* "Where am I coming from?"
*Answer:* "I'm feeling like it's too hard."
*Question:* "Where am I coming from?"
*Answer:* "I'm coming from a place that feels like I might fail or I might not be good enough."

*Question:* "Where am I coming from?"
*Answer:* "I'm afraid I'm going to fail."
*Question:* "Where am I coming from?"
*Answer:* "I'm afraid that I'm just not good enough."

In this example, the belief that says "I'm not good enough" is the bottom line.

**STEP 4**: Once you have come to your bottom line obstruction and written it on the page, put down your pen and acknowledge yourself for your willingness to connect with this part of yourself.

## THE WAY PAST OBSTRUCTION IS *THROUGH* IT

Look over what you have written in the previous two exercises. Notice that *all* of that material is obstruction. All of it is subtext—scripts that we adhere to, for the most part, subconsciously. Having identified many of your obstructions, you can now recognize them whenever they show up in the future. Rather than giving away your power to obstruction, you can see it for what it is. You will know its function and why it is there. That is the start to being able to deal with obstruction effectively.

The way out of obstruction becomes clearer every time you do the following three things:

- **Own it.** Recognize and acknowledge your obstructive behaviors and thought patterns.
- **Understand it.** Know what the obstruction is and understand the purpose it fulfills.
- **Understand yourself.** Understand that the obstruction is coming from a part of you that is afraid of your greatness. Love that aspect of yourself in the same way that you would love a small child who is frightened or has misbehaved.

One of the most powerful practices I know for productively facing and freeing ourselves from obstruction is known simply as The Work. Created by Byron Katie, teacher and author of *Loving What Is*, The Work is a process that involves four questions for unmasking and repro-gramming our obstructions.

## The Work—A Self-Inquiry and Journaling Practice

**STEP 1:** Bring to mind the obstruction that you would like to move beyond. Is it procrastination, judgments and self-criticism, self-doubt, being overwhelmed, losing focus, perfectionism, or another form of obstruction? And what does that voice of obstruction say? Here are a few examples to help clarify your limiting statement:

*"I'll never get past this habit of procrastination."*

*"I'm not capable; I don't have what it takes to succeed."*

*"I have failed before. I'll probably fail again."*

*"Nobody will want what I have to offer."* . . . etc.

**STEP 2:** Take the limiting statement that you just identified through the following four questions:

*Question 1:* Is it true? (Yes or no. If no, move to question 3.) Is it really true? In other words, are you *always* obstructing, procrastinating, screwing up, or whatever your particular story says? Do you ever flow? Do you ever follow through?

*Question 2:* Can you absolutely know that it's true? (Yes or no.) Can you really know that it's true that you obstruct or procrastinate or whatever it is? As you ask yourself this question, remember that absolute knowledge is awfully hard to pin down.

*Question 3:* How do you react—what happens—when you believe that thought? How do you react when you believe the thought that you always procrastinate or you always get sleepy or you always do what-ever you do that is your form of obstruction? Focus on the physical sensations you experience when you have the thought. What happens to your breathing? What happens in your stomach, your shoulders, your back, etc.?

*Question 4:* Who would you be without the thought? Who would you be without the thought that you always procrastinate or always get sleepy or are never in the mood to do your creative work, etc.? What would it be like if you let that thought go?

These four questions are total game changers. Come back to them whenever you need to get past an obstruction. They can help you to figure out the beliefs and perceptions that are limiting you or causing you pain. Whether I'm working alone, with a film crew, an organization, or an individual, the first response to obstruction is usually, "I can't!" Whenever I encounter this heels-dug-in certainty, I find that Katie's questions are a powerful resource, as they were for a CEO who sought my advice when he hit a painful wall.

This highly successful executive was having a conflict with his wife. Accustomed to running a large corporation, he acted like he was at the helm of his married life, too. Refusing to acknowledge that being the CEO at home was causing a rift in his marriage, he was adamant: "I am how I am. I don't know any other way. I'm not capable of re-creating or changing who I fundamentally am." With that, I guided the chief through the four questions.

- He sincerely questioned the assertion that he was "not capable of changing his behaviors" and admitted that it might be untrue.
- He realized that he could not know with absolute certainty if his thoughts about himself were valid.
- He felt rigid, sad, and hopeless about the future when he believed that he was incapable of changing.
- Without the limiting thought, he imagined that he would be more responsive to his wife, open and flexible, and that he would feel "a lot more free."

When we first started working together, I was reminded of the old saying, "To a hammer, everything looks like a nail." He realized that he didn't have to be a hammer in every situation, and his wife emerged as someone he could respond to differently.

In a sense, when we utilize these brilliant questions, we are asking ourselves, "What if I'm willing to be wrong about myself in the pursuit of something new? What if I'm willing to be wrong in the pursuit of something that I think is *right*?" Questions like these calibrate us to handle life in innovative ways.

## GETTING TO THE HEART OF THE MATTER

As essential as psychological processes and awareness practices are for dealing with obstruction, there are times to bypass what can become mental overfunctioning and address obstruction with and through the heart.

The following technique is a simple yet powerful tool that I learned from my friends at the Institute of HeartMath, a heart-science research center. It is a practice that balances thinking with feeling, creating what is called heart-mind coherence. Use this anytime that you feel obstruction or stress.

## Heart Lock-In Technique

STEP 1: Find a peaceful place to relax for five to ten minutes. Close your eyes, take a breath, and shift your attention to the area of your heart.

STEP 2: Imagine that you are breathing slowly through your heart . . . breathing in and out with ease.

STEP 3: While you continue breathing through your heart, recall a feeling of love or appreciation. Maybe it is for a loved one or a pet, or the smell of fresh cookies or jasmine in the springtime.

**STEP 4**: Imagine that you are gently sending out that heart feeling—that appreciation or love—to yourself and others.

**STEP 5**: Continue this transmission from your heart for the full five to ten minutes (or more, if you would like). As thoughts come in, gently return to your heart.

When you feel complete, bring your attention back to your center and slowly open your eyes.

The Heart Lock-In Technique is not only a powerful way to deal with obstruction in the moment but also an equally powerful way to repattern your neural maps from what is familiar and comfortable to something totally new. Because energy follows attention, the more that you feed attention to these new brain maps, the easier it is to access them, and the more quickly the old maps atrophy and dissolve, clearing the path for your creativity to flourish.

## OVERCOMING OBSTRUCTION WITH COURAGE AND COMMITMENT

You can't just power your way through obstruction. Contrary to the Nike philosophy, you can't "just do it." We are hardwired to the way things have been. So attempting to *just do it*, to muscle through, can quickly become another frustrating face of struggle and obstruction. To overcome obstruction takes courage—the word itself derived from the French word *le coeur,* meaning the heart. Thus, moving through obstruction requires heart-mind coherence. In other words, it takes a little acceptance and love.

It also takes commitment.

You can replace the same commitment to struggle with a commitment to courage. You demonstrate courage every time you move ahead in spite of fears, doubts, and other forms of inertia. It takes a big heart to continue to work in spite of—and at the same time aware of—the part of you that is frightened. It takes courage to take the next creative step when some part of you that doesn't believe in itself is vying for your attention.

Creative people know that the hardest part is sitting down to work. But when the willingness to create is met by the will to act in the face of fear, miraculous things occur.

> *You can replace the commitment to struggle with a commitment to courage.*

## THE COURAGE TO KNOW YOURSELF

I received an email from a Catholic nun who teaches at a renewal center in Texas for clergy and other religious women and men. She said that my work resonated with her and she had begun to share something I call "The Three Stories" with her groups. To start off, Sister Lois gave everyone a quick overview of the three stories, distinct stages of creative development.

The first story is always: *Am I creating enough?* A mostly unconscious drive, the question relates primarily to our basic needs. *Am I creating enough food, attention, comfort, things, money, validation, etc.?*

The second story occupies a tremendous amount of our time and mental energy: *Is what I'm creating good enough?* Never fully confident and always with an air of longing, that question keeps us striving and competing. *Is my job, spouse, education, house, car, musical composition, painting, etc., good enough?*

The third story is a revelation: *My creativity IS enough.* My strengths, gifts, talents, skills, and abilities are exactly *enough* to perfectly express the being that *I AM.*

*Enough.*

In the third story, creativity is practiced without any underlying intention to receive validation from self or others. It is a mature relationship with creativity itself.

Once Sister Lois had presented this synopsis, she asked everyone to list the characteristics of their first story, focusing on where they were most concerned with having and creating enough. Then she had them list the characteristics of their second story, outlining where and how they struggle to be good enough; how they attempt to overcome their imagined obstructions, limitations, or lack. Immediately, people asked if they could read aloud from their lists. After a rich period of sharing, they were all inspired to add to their stories after hearing what others had to say. Sister Lois concluded by asking everyone to write a few sentences about their third stories and share with the group again.

You may want to grab a few sheets of paper and do the same. Notice the stories of doing, being, having, and creating *enough* that run through your psyche. See what happens when a commitment to explore the three stages of creative awareness merges with the courage to know that you, and everything that you create, are enough.

# CHAPTER 9

## *Emotional Mastery*

*The artist is a receptacle for emotions
that come from all over the place: from the sky,
from the earth, from a scrap of paper,
from a passing shape, from a spider's web.*
—PABLO PICASSO

You did it. You have arrived at the other side of the creative wall. Having faced creative blocks head-on, you can now turn on the faucet of your creative flow.

The most skilled creators I know are fully aware that creative flow is tied to their emotions. They are also masters of their emotions and have discovered the following recipe for creative aliveness:

- They feel their emotions.
- They let their emotions go once they have felt them.
- Then they choose and feel new emotions.

Emotions are the wellspring of creativity. As you reconnect with imagination, feeling, and being, you will have greater access to that well.

When you have trouble discerning your emotions, what is it that is stopping you? As with creative blocks, fear is often at play when you are experiencing a limited range of emotions. Many people are terrified to feel certain emotions. That was absolutely true for me, hence the obsessive thinking and anxiety that I mistook for feelings when I was younger. For a long time, I felt safer being numb to my emotions and my body. I held many misconceptions about emotions and labeled them positive and negative, and then critically judged the "negative" ones.

## MOVING BEYOND GOOD AND BAD

Whether you have so-called positive or so-called negative emotions, you need to feel them and then let them go. Happy or sad, expansive or restrictive, they need to be discharged. When you don't feel an emotion, or when you deny or repress emotions, they have an unproductive, unhealthy impact on your creativity and well-being in general.

Any emotion or feeling that you feel intensely and then let go of is positive.

Emotions will rise to a crescendo and then dissipate and fall away all by themselves (without exerting any creativity-draining control), if you let them move through you. Don't hold on to them. It is by *feeling* and then *releasing* your emotions that you make them positive.

## BE HERE NOW—UNDERSTANDING INTENSITY

To a creator, the only emotions that are negative are emotions that are not felt and released. And you need to feel your emotions intensely. I don't mean that you have to create teeth-gritting drama or semihysteria. You don't want to ruminate on the past or dwell obsessively on future scenarios. But when you feel intensely, you are fully in the now, in the present, in the present tense—*in-tense*.

Another perspective for dealing with obstructions, scary emotions, and difficult experiences when they arise is to see them collectively as a tinderbox of creativity—they can fire up your creative resources. Use them as fuel, not only to create art but also to create your life as a work of art.

> *To a creator, the only emotions that are negative*
> *are emotions that are not felt and released.*

## FROM IDENTIFYING TO RELATING—THE PATH OF EMOTIONAL MASTERY

At one time or another, everyone has felt consumed by an emotion. We have feared being consumed by an emotion if we dropped our guard. Sadness, anger, and fear are just a few of the emotions that we try to suppress or overcome. But learning how to have a *relationship* with these emotions is far more powerful than overcoming them.

When you identify with an emotion, you can find yourself feeling trapped. It's as if you can't shake off a particular feeling because it is adhered to your sense of self. But when you are having a relationship with an emotion, you are free to take those three magical steps that lead to emotional mastery: *experience it, say good-bye to it, and then choose something else.*

For example, if I'm feeling a lot of fear, I can either identify with the fear and believe that the fear is me or I can experience it as an emotion that is moving through me. The fear is separate from me, and I am in relationship with it. I can feel it fully, notice if it has any information for me, and let it go. If I refuse to let it go, then I can be sure that I am identified with it.

When you believe that emotions tell a negative story about who you are, you may wrestle with them rather than allowing them to move through you.

## CHOOSING VIBRATIONAL STATES

As creators, we have an opportunity to tap into an entirely different relationship with emotions—an *ultracreative* relationship. Understanding emotions as frequencies that create vibrational states, or energy states, is the starting point of this new relationship. Again, one of the keys to being in relationship with our vibrational state is to fully feel what comes up and allow it to dissipate. The other key is to then choose the vibrational state we want to amplify next. If I want a hot shower, I turn the faucet to hot. If I want a cooler shower, I turn the faucet toward the cold side. To make it comfortable, I mix the two. I choose. And the same is true with my vibrational state, my energy.

In other words, to master our emotions is to develop a mastery at choosing our vibrational state. But there is no choice available until we first fully experience the emotional and energetic response we are having. With practice, we can become artists of choosing. The exercises to follow will help you to strengthen your ability to choose.

## INTO THE GARDEN

One of my favorite techniques for practicing the ability to feel an emotion and let it go is called "Into the Garden of Thoughts and Feelings." It is a powerful tool for stirring up new neural connections and new emotions, for cultivating the heart-mind coherence that the Institute of HeartMath teaches.

The secret to how this exercise works is this: Emotions are always tied to thoughts, and thoughts are always tied to emotions. Together, they create this magic called creativity. To get a visceral sense of this, imagine that you are pulling carrots and weeds from a garden bed. When you pull on the leafy greens, a root will always come up. Similarly, when you pull on a thought, a feeling will be there, and when you pull up a feeling, a thought will be there.

Before you begin, refer to the Vocabulary of Feelings in Chapter 4 (page 36). Randomly pick two emotions from the list and then make your way into the garden of thoughts and feelings.

# Into the Garden of Thoughts and Feelings

*PART I*

Find a comfortable place to relax, and take a few centering breaths.

**Emotion #1:** _____

Focusing on the first emotion you chose from the list, feel that emotion as intensely as you can. Feel it, feel it, and feel it some more. As you steep yourself in this feeling, pay attention to the thoughts that come up. If the thought is "nothing is coming up," then that is your thought. The connection between thoughts and feelings is not always logical, so just allow yourself to be aware of whatever comes up.

And then let all of that go.

**Emotion #2:** _____

In the same way, focus on the second emotion. Feel it, feel it . . . and keep feeling it. As you do this, pay attention to the thoughts that arise. Just notice them, even if they don't make perfect sense to you.

And let all of that go.

*PART II*

Now, turn it around and put thoughts first. You can practice with the thoughts provided below or you can choose different thoughts.

**Thought #1:** Your Favorite Holiday

What happens when you think of your favorite holiday? Go, think. Keep thinking of your favorite holiday until a feeling comes up. Let yourself feel that feeling with intensity.

Then let the thought and feeling go.

**Thought #2:** Your Job or Business

Focus like a laser on your job or the business you run. *Think, think, think.* Keep thinking of your work until a feeling comes up. What is the feeling? Feel it, feel it, and feel it some more.

Then let it all go.

Come back to center, taking a deep breath in and gently letting it out.

This technique is a workout. Can you feel it? It does for your creative muscles what going to the gym does for your abs. I recommend spending time in this creativity gym regularly, doing this exercise as a practice. It pays dividends that are astonishing. Your emotional fitness will show up as an intimacy with your feelings and your thinking, where you give care and attention to both.

The next exercise is a practice for finding the gold inside of the feelings and emotions that you might consider to be "bad" or negative in some way. You will find that tremendous creative power has been locked away inside your anxiety, fear, frustration, anger, or resentment.

## Discovering Hidden Creativity— A Meditative Journaling Exercise

Find a quiet place to reflect inwardly and to write.

Take a few minutes to connect with yourself, focusing on your breathing and allowing yourself to relax.

STEP 1: On a scale from 1 to 10, how would you rate your emotional energy? The number 1 represents feeling constricted in some way, and the number 10 represents feeling open and connected. The numbers in between represent various levels of limitation or flow you may be experiencing. Starting exactly where you are, choose your number.

STEP 2: Write a paragraph or two about what you are feeling in this moment. Describe the accompanying physical sensation(s). Perhaps you feel a tightness, tingling, pulsing, or pinching. I often experience a tightness across the chest or stiffness in my neck. Even if the sensation is a numbness or emptiness, that counts, too.

**STEP 3**: Imagine that these sensations are connected to the emotions you described in Step 1. Your job is to figure out how they are connected. Spend a few minutes writing about the connection.

Moving on to the thoughts that are connected to your feelings, emotions, and physical sensations . . .

**STEP 4**: Describe your mental state. For example, notice if your thoughts have to do with blame or running away or punishing or judging or comparing yourself to someone. Take a few minutes to write about what is going on in your head.

**STEP 5**: On a scale from 1 to 10, rate your creative energy now—with number 1 representing heavy or low energy, number 10 representing high energy or a lightening up, and the numbers between representing variations along the scale. Having acknowledged and expressed your thoughts and feelings, do you notice a change? Choose your number and write a paragraph or two describing what you sense happening with your creative energy.

As you do these two practices regularly, you are training yourself to creatively express and then release your thoughts, feelings, and emotions. You are transcending the need to label them as positive or negative now that you know how to work with them. Each time you do so, you are further developing your CQ—the creativity quotient that is all about frequencies, all about emotions . . . all about the underlying qualitative generosity of heart and spirit.

For many years, whenever I was under stress, I had a tendency to cut off from myself and my ability to feel. It often looked like this: sitting with a friend "on autopilot" and realizing that I had no feelings whatsoever about what they were saying. By practicing these exercises, I learned to catch these lapses and come back to my aliveness.

An actor I worked with told me within the first minute that he was "a major workaholic." As we talked about his life, it became evident that he constantly put aside his feelings. Not only did he ignore his subtler feelings, but he also ignored his basic body sensations and needs, like eating when he was hungry or going to sleep when he was tired. As a result of these two exercises, a light went on. He realized that he was treating himself as an object, and that he approached the thoughts and feelings of others with the same insensitivity as he did his own. His creative life, health, relationships—all were missing his presence and care. These were painful moments of reckoning for him, but he stuck with the practices and things turned around. Thoughts and feelings took on new meaning and richness for him. As he discovered new responses, others found him to be more open and available.

A change of heart is often a matter of *capacity*. If your capacity to relate to your own feelings is limited, you will feel emotionally disconnected from others. You can't create a connection with another person greater than the emotional intimacy you have with yourself. If you are a parent, spouse, or friend, this understanding could make all the difference in the life of someone you love.

## CHAPTER 10

# *Engaging the Muses:*
# *Stepping into Creative Flow*

*The object isn't to make art, it's to be in that wonderful state*
*which makes art inevitable.*
—ROBERT HENRI

One of the most rewarding projects of my career is a feature-length documentary called *When I Was Young I Said I Would Be Happy*, which tells of the emotional healing of twelve orphaned genocide survivors in Rwanda. Recovering from post-traumatic stress disorder (PTSD), these young people are paying it forward by working with others who have also experienced the unthinkable. They are transforming their own despair and grief into compassion in action, including in places like Newtown, Connecticut, where twenty children and six adults were murdered at Sandy Hook Elementary School.

One shining example is the young Rwandan woman who worked via Skype with an eleven-year-old boy in Newtown. His caregivers and mental health professionals had been unreachable to him, but soon after he began work with the Rwandan woman, the boy was able to go back to school. He expressed his feelings by raising enough money at his new school to send the young woman to four years of college. A veritable loop of healing and love had been set in motion.

When I was sure I had finished the documentary, I showed it to some filmmakers and friends in order to get their critiques.

"You're not done," they said. "It's dragging in the middle."

I didn't enjoy hearing it, but I knew in my gut they were right.

When my film editor expressed her frustration, it mirrored my own. We bickered and griped, but eventually we went back to work. We cut six minutes. Then another two minutes. Finally a few more.

That's when something special happened.

Suddenly the muse kicked in, and we created a whole new scene from footage that we hadn't paid much attention to, focused on a young Rwandan scholar who is supported in his education by contributions from a classroom of kids in Pacific Grove, California. The Californians huddle together for a Skype call with the young student in Rwanda. The students reach across the miles with their caring, and the tenderness and excitement is visceral. In the end, it wasn't only a matter of cutting to make things shorter. Guided by the muse, an opportunity arose to add emotional texture and depth that drove the story forward. When we showed the documentary again, it felt complete to everyone . . . and the new scene became one of the most powerful in the movie.

When we take action, even in the face of inner confusion and outer obstacles, we invoke the muses. They are the mysterious helpers who have the power to replace doubt with curiosity, and obstruction with inspiration.

Whether throwing clay on a pottery wheel or writing a business manifesto, as creators come to discover, we all need a little help sometimes.

> *When we take action, even in the face of inner confusion*
> *and outer obstacles, we invoke the muses.*

## OUR UNSEEN ALLIES—THE OLYMPIAN NINE

For thousands of years, artists and creators of all kinds have invoked the muses for knowledge and guidance. *The Odyssey*, Homer's epic poem from the eighth century BC, begins with just such an invocation, a request for aid and assistance in telling the great tale: "Sing in me, Muse, and through me tell the story . . ."

Unabashedly, the narrator asks to be used as a vessel of creative expression.

Historically known as the Olympian Nine, the muses are nine distinct goddesses of Greek mythology: Thalia, Clio, Calliope, Terpsichore, Melpomene, Erato, Euterpe, Polyhymnia, Urania. They are the creative powers that desire to help us express, build, and make the things that matter to us. They are the unseen allies that inspire—*in-spirit*—creators.

As you see their names, or as you sound them out, some may already seem familiar to you. As you learn about their specific areas of genius and guidance, notice if feelings, images, or memories are stirred by one or more of the muses.

## THE MUSES—AND HOW TO WORK WITH THEM

When exploring the muses, don't be misled by the word *mythology*. The muses are not relics of a made-up, ancient world. They are creative forces outside the bounds of our structured imagining; each one is vibrantly and imaginatively alive. Like the forces of nature, they can be called on to grow the garden of our ideas, thoughts, and feelings.

*Thalia begins the awakening with Innocence and Humor.* She says, Take a chance. Try something new. Taste something new. Listen to the radio in a language you don't understand. Be willing to laugh at all the things you do for love without remembering you are loved all along.

*Clio is the Muse of History and Tradition.* She expands our awakening by placing it in perspective. She says, Explore your own history and tradition. Recall family stories, heirlooms, and souvenirs. Make art out of your memory and experience.

*Calliope is the voice of The Call, the heroic voice.* Her voice rises above the clamor and signals an awakening that is about to become transforming. She asks, What are you called to? Where have you wandered? What is your S/Hero's Journey or Great Work? Garden, cook, write, create to express your thoughts and feelings about where you are going.

*Terpsichore is the Muse of Movement.* After we awaken, in order to transform, we must move. Terpsichore inspires us to move, to act. What can you *do* today? Play? Dance? Collaborate? Create? You can't move a parked car, she says. Whatever it is, DO IT.

*Melpomene is the Muse of Dignity and also of Tragedy.* She invites you to show up as the Hero or S/hero of your life. She can be called on to face adversity with courage, and to be strong enough to feel your feelings without clinging to them. She says: Comfort others by example. Reach out to neighbors in pain. Sing and write in honor of another. Above all, be optimistic. Always.

*Erato is the Muse of Love, Compassion, Eros, Libido, and Friendship.* Hers is the voice of emotion. She says: Create a meal, story, or a gesture for another person. What can you give that comforts, inspires, or arouses the heart of another? Whatever it is, give it.

*Euterpe is the Muse of Music and Intuition.* Music restores, provokes, and stimulates. She encourages: Listen for music everywhere—street sounds, the drip of the kitchen faucet, children at play. Follow hunches. A hunch is the subtle voice of Euterpe. She is trying to reach you.

*Polyhymnia is the Muse of Symbolism and sacred choral music.* She is often associated with the music of pure tone, such as the music of the flute. She says, Listen to music of pure tones, or sit in silence and allow any thoughts and feelings to bubble up from your unconscious mind. Pay attention to the symbols and metaphors. Recall a dream. Write it down. Figure out what it might mean.

*Urania is the Muse of the sacred One Voice (Uni-Verse or Making One) and of all celestial things.* She says, Be curious about everything you experience, especially if it feels familiar. Look for what is new. Your job is to figure out how everything is interconnected.

## BEING IN THE FLOW

Once you engage with them, the muses will cocreate with you 24/7, but only as long as you remain committed. They respond to sincerity and constancy. Even when your conscious attention is not focused on the work ahead, they are churning away, working with your subconscious intelligence in its various forms. You feel an ease and an elegance when you remember that you don't have to "go it alone." Calling on the muses is a powerful way to get into the creative flow.

## FOSTERING A RELATIONSHIP WITH THE MUSES THROUGH RITUAL AND TECHNIQUE

The muses wait to be invited. Beyond any words we speak, it is the willingness to move in spite of obstruction, to act even when we have hit a creative speed bump, that the muses receive as an invitation. Procrastination, perfectionism, exhaustion, distraction, writer's block—when we are willing cocreators, the muses can handle them all.

*Establish Routine.* Determine a set time for your creative work, as well as a set place. It could be a daily commitment to 7:00 a.m., 3:00 in the afternoon, or midnight; whatever time is in sync with your natural inclinations and rhythms. Maybe what works best for you is to commit to three or four sessions each week at the exact same time.

*Arrange Your Workspace with Love and Care.* Adorn it with the colors, textures, and objects that spark your imagination and connect you with your emotions. You might find certain pieces of music to be an important part of your setting. With intention and attention, design an environment for your creativity that has a refreshing and enlivening tone.

Find out what happens when you keep your commitment to that time and place.

*Movement and Rhythm.* Creative *qi*, or energy, is released when you move your body and wake up your neural connections through rhythm and motion, even in subtle ways. You don't have to do an elaborate trance dance to invite the muses. Sway to the music of the washing machine or dishwasher. Breathe with the wind chimes. Move to the drumming of raindrops on your roof or the birdsong outside your window. You can find many creative connections as you simply sit at your desk.

*Priming the Pump.* Writing techniques are often keys to unlocking doors of consciousness for the muses to enter. Whether you are searching for a creative solution to a challenge, seeking to clarify the next step in your project, or hoping for a wave of inspiration to sweep you off your feet, any one of these will serve you.

## Warming Up to the Muses—Timed Writings

With an egg timer or alarm clock, set your desired time for spontaneous, nonstop writing on any subject; three to five minutes is plenty. For example, write about how you feel about work, or being out in nature, or your newfound love of French wines. Or choose two unrelated subjects and look for the connection between them, like the pear tree in your backyard and your neighbor's silver RV.

At a certain point, you will automatically trigger the assistance of the muses. Out of the blue, an idea comes—and another. All of a sudden, you are pushing through in spite of fear, doubt, and obstructions of any kind.

For a creative twist, try spontaneous writing with your nondominant hand. If you are right-handed, use your left hand and vice versa. See what happens when you approach your feelings, problems, and solutions that way.

### The Brain Dump

Akin to brainstorming, the Brain Dump is a fertile starting point for any creative project.

*The requirement.* You need to be willing to let your inner censor take a break. Just as you would suspend criticism of a child who is sharing an idea with you or showing you an art project, wide-eyed with innocence, suspend all criticism of yourself.

*Hold nothing back.* This is an opportunity to pour out your initial ideas, feelings, images, words, or inklings without concern for what you might *do* with them next. Let them flow forth . . . onto the page or the canvas, into the recording device, or wherever they are best captured.

**Honor humble beginnings.** There are websites, such as theatlantic .com and flavorwire.com, where you can access first drafts of some of the classic works of literature. You can see the first handwritten pages of *The Adventures of Huckleberry Finn*, early line edits of *Madame Bovary*, and other optimistic points of departure. Some of our most beloved movies, plays, songs, and works of art started as bits and pieces of loosely formed ideas barely strung together. If you are ever dreaming up a book title, or a title for anything at all, it might be comforting to learn that Tolstoy's *War and Peace* was originally titled *All's Well That Ends Well*, and Steinbeck's *Of Mice and Men* started off as *Something That Happened*. These are humble first steps. Refining our ideas comes later.

## Vaporizing the Critics

This practice is my preferred way to deal with the voices of obstruction, especially my internal judges, whom I call my critics. Freeing myself from the critics creates an internal space (a quieter space) for the muses to come forth.

Close your eyes, relax, and take yourself through the following sequence.

STEP 1: Recall an occasion where you felt judged by someone, either in the past or more recently. Re-experience the feeling in detail. See who is judging you and hear what he or she is saying (or what you believe they "must be" thinking).

Notice how that feels.

STEP 2: Once you have a vivid sense of this experience, create a way to "vaporize" that person in your imagination. It could be via a ray gun, an explosive, or an ejection chair that jettisons the critic right out of your reality; it's your choice. Go ahead and use your "vaporizer."

**STEP 3**: Feel how it is to be free from the critic. How does your body feel? How does your heart feel? What do you sense on the emotional level? Has anything changed in the space around you?

When you feel complete, take a deep breath and slowly open your eyes.

Creative relief can be found by acknowledging that, yes, obstruction will come up, but it doesn't need to hinder you. Utilize these practices and *something* will move.

## MAKING CONTACT WITH THE MUSES

Which of these forces would you like to call on for inspiration? Thalia, Clio, Calliope, Terpsichore, Melpomene, Erato, Euterpe, Polyhymnia, or Urania? What qualities touch your creative soul at this moment in time?

Innocence and Humor

History, Tradition, and Memory

The Call to Your Great Work

Movement and Action

Dignity, Optimism, and Courage in the Face of Adversity

Love, Compassion, and Eros

Music and Intuition

Symbolism, Metaphor, and the Pure Musical Tones of Your Unconscious, or . . .

The Sacred One Voice that Speaks of the Interconnection of all Things

Let your finger land on one of these lines. Trust the creative desire that courses through your heart and hands. Reach toward the muse that is sending a signal your way today.

# *Try This!*

## TAPPING FOR CREATIVITY

I learned the technique referred to as "tapping" from my colleague Nick Ortner, creator of the Tapping Summit. As another antidote to obstructions and a method for opening to creative flow, tapping is a powerfully effective tool.

Tapping is based on the Chinese meridian energy system, so you use your fingertips to lightly tap various spots located on the face and upper body that correlate to emotions. Tapping is sometimes referred to as emotional acupuncture.

As you move through the nine tapping positions in this exercise, I will guide you incrementally through the following statement:

"As I create my _____ (novel, screenplay, relationship, business plan, sculpture, website, etc.), my attention is committed. Everything that I experience is held forever in my subconscious mind and is accessible to me. I desire all the resources and information I need to accomplish my goal of _____ (novel, screenplay, relationship, business plan, sculpture, website, etc.) for the purpose of _____ (inspiring others, creating fulfillment, having fun, etc.)."

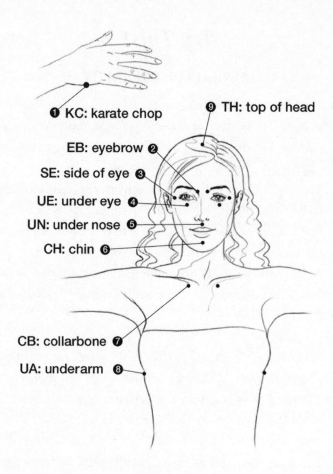

❶ KC: karate chop

❾ TH: top of head

EB: eyebrow ❷

SE: side of eye ❸

UE: under eye ❹

UN: under nose ❺

CH: chin ❻

CB: collarbone ❼

UA: underarm ❽

Select your side: If you are right-handed, use the fingertips of the middle three fingers of your right hand. If you are left-handed, use the fingertips of the middle three fingers of your left hand.

How many taps is enough? I rely on the Goldilocks factor: Tapping on each spot fewer than three times may not be enough and more than five is probably too much. So three to five times is just about right. Just find your own sweet spot . . . and tap, tap, tap.

*1st position:* Begin tapping lightly on the karate chop part of your left hand, or on that part of your right hand if you're left-handed. If you were splitting a board with the side of your hand, it's the part that would hit the board first. While you are tapping on the karate chop point, you are going to repeat the following statement: "As I create my _____ (novel, screenplay, relationship, painting, website, etc. . . .)"

*Note: The continuation of your statement will happen incrementally with the remaining eight tapping positions.*

*2nd position:* Move to the second point, tapping with both hands at the inside edge of your eyebrows, toward the bridge of your nose. Tap, tap, tap, repeating the same statement, "As I create my _____ (novel, screenplay, relationship, painting, website, etc.) . . ."

*3rd position:* Move to the third point, tapping with both hands at the outside corner of the eyes, just before the temple. Tap, tap, tap, repeating the following statement: ". . . my attention is committed, my attention is committed, my attention is committed."

*4th position:* Move to the fourth position, tapping with both hands right under the eyes, in the center of the bone. Tap, tap, tap, repeating this statement: "Everything that I experience, everything that I experience, everything that I experience . . ."

*5th position:* Under the nose, tap with one or both hands on the spot right between the bottom of your nose and your top lip. Tap, tap, tap as you complete the above statement: ". . . is held forever in my subconscious mind, held forever in my subconscious mind, held forever in my subconscious mind . . ."

*6th position:* Move to the sixth position, tapping with one or both hands just above the chin, in the fold between the bottom lip and the chin. Tap, tap, tap while continuing the statement: ". . . and is accessible to me, is accessible to me, is accessible to me."

*7th position:* At the seventh position, tap on the center of your collarbone. Here you can tap with one hand on one collarbone or both hands on both collarbones. Tap, tap, tap, repeating this statement: "I desire all the resources and information I need, desire all the resources and information I need, desire all the resources and information I need . . ."

*8th position:* Tap under one arm (it can be under your left arm or your right arm). For women, it is right at the bra line, and for men, it's one hand's width under the armpit. Tap, tap, tap, completing the statement started above: ". . . to accomplish my goal of _____, to accomplish my goal of _____, to accomplish my goal of _____ (referring to the creative goal you started with in the first position)."

*9th and last position:* The last position is at the top of the head, at the crown point. Tap, tap, tap gently with one or both hands at the center of your head, stating the purpose of your creative endeavor.

Examples:

"*For the purpose of inspiring others, inspiring others, inspiring others.*"

*"For the purpose of creating fulfillment, creating fulfillment, creating fulfillment."*

*"For the purpose of having fun, having fun, having fun."*

Completion: After you have finished the sequence, take a deep breath and release it.

Repeat this technique as needed and desired.

# CHAPTER 11

## *Image Making*

*Human beings are not born once and for all
on the day their mothers give birth to them . . .
life obliges them over and over again
to give birth to themselves.*
—GABRIEL GARCÍA MÁRQUEZ

We are wired for aliveness, built to experience, taste, touch, give, share, and express the unique pulse of life that courses through our veins. We are fully equipped to create and manifest success. So why do we sometimes miss the boats of opportunity that come into port—opportunities for advancement, to cocreate with others, or to otherwise share our skills, talents, and gifts?

To answer this question, we can look to our classic Western movies with stars like John Wayne or Gary Cooper. There is always the scene where the rugged hero breaks the wild mustang. He runs down the stallion (always a stallion) and lassos it out of the herd. Then he throws a saddle onto the horse's back while it bucks, kicks, and twists like crazy. At first, the guy gets tossed like a salad, but in the end it's no contest. The horse quits fighting. With our hero tall in the saddle, the horse's lightning-fast gallop has become a docile walk. He has been "broken." Fast-forward a few months or years later, the stallion is following the hero around like a baby duckling behind its mother.

What is going on? The stallion is bigger, stronger, and faster. Why doesn't he make a break for the open range? What holds him back?

The secret is *image*.

The stallion's experience of being saddle-broken shapes his response to all the breakout opportunities of life. He is a prisoner of his *image*.

## WHAT IS IMAGE?

Image is who and what we imagine ourselves to be. It is also what we put out there for others to experience of us—what we show the world.

As you grow, your image needs to grow, too. If you create more but do not change your image, it will not hold who you are becoming, or what you are creating.

This is critical to understand. If you cannot imagine yourself in new ways, if you can't imagine yourself creative or happy, successful or deserving, *then you will always shrink back to fit into your old image.* As a creator, it is imperative that you become skillful at creating an expanded image.

## HOW DO YOU SEE YOURSELF?

Sometimes I ask people to describe themselves with only three adjectives. They might say, "Well, you know, I am friendly, I'm tenacious, I'm loyal." Or, "I'm loving, hardworking, disappointed in love." Or, "I am a successful person, a romantic, and always restless." They say volumes in just a few words.

It is now your turn to get clear about who you imagine yourself to be.

### Three Adjectives Technique

Describe yourself to a prospective new employer, your dream date, or to a publisher who is considering your novel. Tell them who you are:

Adjective #1 _____

Adjective #2 _____

Adjective #3 _____

***Your body as messenger.*** Review your three adjectives, sensing each one in your body. *Feel* them in your body. What kind of sensations do you register? Do you feel a flutter in your stomach? Tightness in your chest? Stiffness in your neck? Do you feel a warmth in your hands or tingling in your head?

_____

_____

_____

_____

_____

_____

_____

***Translating the messages.*** What is the connection between the feelings in your body and your three adjectives? Take three minutes to write down what the sensations in your body are telling you. Trust the first ideas that come to you.

Some questions to consider as you write: Do you believe how you have described yourself, or does something there feel like a stretch? Are you especially excited and inspired by something you wrote down? Is there a descriptor you would prefer to change? Allow yourself to be completely honest for the purpose of your creative growth.

_____

_____

_____

_____

_____

_____

_____

_____

_____

_____

_____

_____

_____

_____

_____

_____

_____

_____

What have you discovered about your self-image so far? How do you see yourself? If you see yourself as successful, others probably will, too. If you see yourself as a winner, you will be a winner in the eyes of others.

What qualities and characteristics would you like to deepen or reclaim? Are you as confident, dependable, or trustworthy (fill in your own desired qualities) as you want to be?

The good news is that it is impossible to project an image that isn't true. We have a built-in integrity mechanism. If we try to spin a wobbly image, then others will experience it as being inauthentic.

If you find that your image is lacking in some way, you must not shrink back from that. You cannot forgive or change what you do not own. After all, you can't give away your house if you don't hold the deed to it.

To unleash your full creative power, it is essential to bring your image fully to light and to create it anew on a regular basis.

Because I keep outgrowing my image, the following technique is one that I revisit frequently.

> *To unleash your full creative power, it is essential
> to bring your image fully to light and to create it anew
> on a regular basis.*

## Image-Making Technique

### PART I—Unmasking the Old Image

Set aside approximately forty-five minutes each for Parts I and II of this free-form writing exercise.

**All about YOU.** For the first thirty minutes, write out every thought and feeling you have regarding your image. It could be your image in general or your image as a creative person—a creator of art, business, good health, or something else that you highly value. It could be your image as a creator of beautiful relationships, money, jobs, or opportunities.

Write about how you *feel* about yourself, what you *think* of yourself, what you *know* about yourself, and how you *see* yourself.

Write and write and write and write. If you get tired, write about the tiredness. Keep writing. When you go off topic, gently steer yourself back to "how do I feel about my image?"

After half an hour, stop. Look over what you have done. You will notice certain words, themes, and ideas that recur. Make note of those or highlight them. They will be useful in the next steps.

**One page.** Distill all the initial writings down to one page.

**One paragraph.** Reduce the one page down to a single paragraph.

**One sentence.** Reduce that one paragraph to one sentence. This sentence is the *essence* of your self-image.

**One word.** Reduce your single sentence to one word. This word represents your image.

### PART II—Constructing the New Image

Write a sentence about *who you are growing into.*

Develop this sentence into a full page.

Next develop the one page into many pages. In other words, keep writing without a pause. When you have written nonstop for at least thirty minutes, stop.

Working backward, distill all the writings to one page, one paragraph, one sentence, one word.

That word is your new image.

Make it real. Feed it with your attention and intention. Think of it as a homeopathic remedy, holding the energy of who you can be. Carry it with you. Tune in to it. Put in on your desk or worktable. Look for anything and everything in your reality to support it.

*In the beginning was the word.*

To integrate this process over time, you can follow up with meditation, prayer, daydreaming, or further journaling. Reflect on your new image. Protect it. Share it only with people who care—a coach, your spouse, a close friend. Express it through the quality of your actions in the world. Pay attention to your feelings and imaginings. Know that each successive refinement of your image will make it more powerful.

## A GREAT SECRET

If or when you encounter obstruction while doing your image work, take heart: *The level and intensity of the obstruction is equal to the level and intensity of the creativity that waits for you on the other side.*

## CHAPTER 12

# *Jump-Starting Vision*

*When a mind is raised, and animated by scenes that engage the heart,*
*then those qualities which would otherwise lay dormant, wake into life . . .*
—ABIGAIL ADAMS, U.S. FIRST LADY

When you look toward your future, what do you see?

Harvard psychology professor David McClellan found that he could predict a person's future from the way he or she daydreamed about the future. He found that successful people created daydreams about their goals—how they went about achieving them and how they felt in the process of reaching them. He also discovered that they picked challenging goals that would give them strong feelings of satisfaction. The professor discovered what highly creative people have known all along: that the *feeling* of achievement is both the goal itself and the secret to creating it.

## WHAT SIGNALS ARE YOU BROADCASTING?

Having a vision for your life is a creative act. When you have vision, you generate a set of energetic frequencies that interact with one another. These create harmonics that send out signals, like broadcast transmissions from a radio station, only these signals are communicating with your future.

As you grow and move forward into that future, your vision becomes the experiences of your life and they show up in the outer world in myriad ways. You essentially meet up with the signals that you have been emitting.

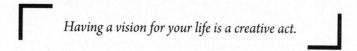

*Having a vision for your life is a creative act.*

## CHOOSING AND ALLOWING— THE TWO CREATIVE PATHWAYS

We are always encountering the outward manifestations that arise from either our conscious creativity or our conditioned creativity— our structured imagining. In other words, everything that happens to us is either directly *chosen* or it is *allowed*. The same is true for how we create.

- We create by consciously choosing *(in alignment with conscious creativity)* or . . .
- we create by allowing *(in alignment with structured imagining)*.

In either case, the combined frequency of our *choices, beliefs,* and *expectations* broadcasts outward. It casts visions into the future that we come to discover in time.

Sometimes we cast visions of wonderful creations when we are younger, forgetting that we ever put them out there in the first place. For example, I didn't know until a few years ago that one of the pleasures of my life would be teaching. Now I enjoy leading seminars and courses on creativity and transformation. When I considered my past recently, I remembered that I was a ski instructor in high school teaching young kids. Teaching gave me tremendous satisfaction. I made the connection between then and now, understanding that the satisfaction I experience today is a familiar friend. I seeded it as a *feeling* many years ago, unconsciously. Yet here I am, discovering the richness of this vision . . . and it is discovering me. I am in relationship with this burgeoning vision.

What future vision is looking for you right now? Is it something you wanted many years ago that you tossed into the field of possibilities with your desire and imagination? Or is a brand-new vision being awakened?

The following techniques will bring this vision to light.

## The Multiple-Times Technique

**STEP 1**: Imagine something you want to create. It could be an online business, a sum of money, a new level of health, a baby, a bestseller, an oil painting, a dance recital—some expression of your creative abundance.

**STEP 2**: Choose a time frame for your creation. Visualize your birthday or a holiday (such as Christmas, Halloween, or New Year's Day) as your marker in time. You are going to achieve your successful outcome by that date.

**STEP 3**: See yourself with your friends and family on this day of celebration, acknowledging and enjoying your success. As you do this, amplify your vision by anchoring the experience to things that vividly evoke your senses. For example:

- Imagine the smell of fall leaves or a freshly squeezed lemon. *Now imagine the smell of your success.*
- Imagine the taste of a hot-from-the-oven chocolate brownie or a spoonful of your favorite ice cream. *Now imagine the taste of your success.*
- Imagine the feel of a soft, purring kitten or a golden lab puppy asleep in your lap. *Now imagine the feel of your success.*

**STEP 4**: Using your imagination, go back into your past. From that vantage point, see yourself having the beginnings that will lead to your future success. What is the logical progression of events and opportunities that will culminate in this creation?

**STEP 5**: Return again to your celebration with loved ones, where you are feeling, understanding, enjoying, and sharing your success.

Playing with time, toggling back and forth between the future and the past with your senses engaged, is an effective practice for activating vision. Now we will apply the same fluidity to *space*.

## The Multiple-Space Technique

The setup: The following example illustrates how this technique can be used to loosen the hold of structured imagining and supercharge a creative vision. In this example, my intention is to set the outcome for an upcoming program scheduled for my weekly Southern California radio show, an episode with a special guest. I want it to be successful.

With eyes closed, I imagine myself seated behind the microphone in the radio studio opposite my regular cohost. I am imagining the scene as if from behind my own eyes, with the desks, mixing board, and control room in front of me. I picture the program on air, seeing with my inner vision the lively exchanges with my cohost and guest. I visualize the scene in minute detail. It's critical that I *feel* it, fully engaged in the conversation and inspired by bringing our listeners a show that is entertaining and informative, one that makes a difference in their lives.

With my senses fired up, I "POP!" outside of myself, viewing the scene from approximately three steps behind and slightly above my body. I pay attention to detail, seeing myself sitting in the chair and engaged in the program. I might POP! back and forth two or three times before swooping finally back into my body, and the view from behind my eyes.

**STEP 1**: Visualize a creation, event, or experience you want to have. This could be the same as the successful outcome you focused on in the previous exercise or something completely different.

**STEP 2**: With your imagination, experience yourself inside of your creation. It is happening and you're looking at it through your physical eyes.

**STEP 3**: Move your awareness backward, popping back two or three steps behind yourself. See your creation from this vantage point.

**STEP 4**: Move your awareness upward. Pop up two or three feet and watch the scene from this perspective.

**STEP 5**: Swooping back down, look at your creation again from behind your eyes.

Do this two or three times, alternating space and perspectives, and sensing the creative power derived from shifting your awareness.

The next technique is one that I learned from my friend Lazaris. This elegant practice has worked well for me over many years. The focus of time is exactly thirty-three seconds, which sets up a window of neural activity for breaking through habituated brain patterns that block your vision.

## The Thirty-Three Second Technique

**STEP 1**: With an egg timer, computer clock, smart phone, or regular alarm clock, set the time for exactly thirty-three seconds.

**STEP 2**: Decide on a single scene, a specific snapshot of something you want to create.

**STEP 3**: Once you have decided on the single scene, start the timer. . . . Put yourself inside the scene and experience it with as much feeling as you can summon. With as much intensity as you can invoke, feel the happiness, joy, elation, peace, enthusiasm, or other uplifting emotions associated with your creation.

**STEP 4:** After holding that intensity for exactly thirty-three seconds, drop it. Completely release the images and feelings. Take a deep breath in and out, letting it all go.

The combination of seeing what you want to create and summoning the associated feelings for that concentrated period of time is a HIGHLY potent recipe for manifestation. For maximum impact, use all three techniques to consciously awaken vision.

## VISION BORN OF COMPASSION

There is vision that we actively seek to awaken, and then there is vision that comes more like a revelation. Sometimes the suffering we experience personally or sense in others awakens compassion. It opens our eyes in ways that change us.

My friend Mikki Willis, founder and CEO of Elevate Films, is one of the most creative people I know, an innovator with a socially conscious mission. Mikki was part of the rescue and cleanup crew at Ground Zero in New York City in the days following the terrorist attacks of September 11, 2001. He had been working for about forty hours straight when he found a couch inside an abandoned apartment building to take a nap on. As he lay there with his eyes closed, he had a vision that changed the course of his life. He understood in an instant that the traumatic nature of the work there could either be his undoing or an opening. The choice was his. As he walked out of the apartment building and into the floodlights where the search continued, he saw the interconnectedness of everyone and everything. "Oneness" was no longer simply a concept. In the midst of the horror and devastation, he was lifted by the beauty of what is possible when we come together. At this demarcation point, Mikki's purpose of creating community came into clear view. In the extremes of human experience, we are often able to bypass the clutter of distractions and get to what really matters.

Sometimes the soul speaks to us through beauty, sometimes through pain. I believe this explains why there is such an outpouring of creative expression from many young men and women on the front lines of war. I call them battlefield poets because inside impossibly difficult circumstances they write letters to their loved ones and communities that are like sonnets of compassion, forgiveness, understanding, and wisdom. In the midst of the brutality, they touch what is beautiful and true.

When we make contact with what matters, creative expression comes unimpeded from our deepest self.

What matters most to you? Was there a difficult moment of pain or suffering in which you experienced a stirring of care and compassion? How might that catalyze your next creative act?

One of the most effective ways to discover a creative vision is to make a *compassionately charged connection* with your younger self.

> *When we make contact with what matters, creative expression comes unimpeded from our deepest self.*

## Discovering a Compassionately Charged Vision— A Timed-Writing Exercise

**Preparations:** With a clock or timer and your journal in hand, set aside five minutes for this exercise. Take a deep breath to center and relax.

**STEP 1—The memory:** In your mind, travel back to the most painful incident of your youth. Look to the period between seven to fifteen years old. There you will find a whole menu of possibilities. Write down the memory in a stream-of-consciousness fashion, allowing the page to fill with the remembrance of that pain.

For me, it was the agony of day camp when I was eight years old. Baseball games were a nightmare for me. I couldn't hit or field the ball. With every lost game, I felt that I alone had cost my team the win. All summer long, my face was perpetually flushed with shame and humiliation.

Give your remembrance a name. It can be as simple as "The Camp Story."

**STEP 2—The meaning:** Look again at your story of pain. What is the meaning that you assigned to yourself and the situation or circumstance?

In my case, "The Camp Story" meant that I was *not good enough*. From that point on, I played small in life, always attempting to be invisible in order to avoid further humiliation and pain. And I stuck to that plan for many years.

**STEP 3—The gift:** Inside your story of pain is a simple lesson or understanding that will catalyze your creativity. Most often it is your unique expression of caring for others born out of a tender remembrance of your own hardship.

After reconnecting with my younger self, I began to regard every interaction as an opportunity to ask myself, "How can I support others to play *large*?" This vision has been the core theme of my creative voice for years.

What is the lesson of your story? The answer to that question is a gift that you are here to give.

# CHAPTER 13

# *Accelerated Creativity: Energies of Creation, Part II*

*If you want to build a ship, don't drum up the men to gather wood,*
*divide the work, and give orders. Instead, teach them to yearn*
*for the vast and endless sea.*
—ANTOINE DE SAINT-EXUPÉRY

Masculine and feminine energies, sometimes called yang and yin, are the two fundamental forces of creativity. Not to be confused with maleness or femaleness, the masculine energies of will and action interact with the feminine energies of receptivity, imagining, feeling, and being. In Chapter 3, we examined what happens when the field of connection between them is interrupted or altogether denied. The crucial balance between doing and being is lost in chauvinism. Without conscious attention, these energies are almost always out of balance. When you can strike that balance, however, the outcomes can be dramatic . . . and capable of changing reality as you know it.

The theory of relativity arrived in a dream state to Albert Einstein, who instinctively engaged both masculine and feminine energies in his subconscious mind, and *imagined* the answer or solution. In his dream that changed our perceptions of space and time, Einstein saw a starry night. He and his friends were sledding down a steep hill. On one particular trip down, he became aware that he was traveling faster and faster. Holding a mirror in front of himself, he saw his reflection moving on a beam of light and realized that the reflection was moving faster than he was. Understanding that the sled was approaching the speed of light, he looked up and saw that the stars had changed in appearance, refracting into a brilliant spectrum of colors he had never seen before that moment. When he woke up, his *analytical* mind kicked in and he went to work on what he had experienced in the dream state.

"I knew I had to understand that dream," he later said. "You could say that my entire scientific career has been a meditation on that dream."

## FROM INSPIRATION TO ACTION

Einstein was also known for playing the violin while he was out sailing. He would give his analytical *doing* mind a rest and simply experience *being*—being in nature, in the elements, in the music, each one a different environment of aliveness. When it was time to return to work, he was refreshed and energetically in balance.

In these moments, Einstein was *inspired*. He was in a receptive state of being where creativity is born. Just as inspiration is a gift, all creativity is a gift from beyond as well. It is a gift delivered to us through our imagination and our feelings. Once the gift is received, we then hand it over to the *doer* aspect of ourselves. The *doer*—the theoretical physicist, the baker, the teacher, the writer, the artist, the go-getter—is always the one who unwraps and unpacks the gift.

After Einstein received the gift of inspiration in the dream, he went to his chalkboard and began computations. He went from a state of receptivity to a state of activity. First we receive the inspiration, then we move into action based on that inspiration. We write the first draft, do the dictation, open up a new spreadsheet, plant the row of seeds, send the file, take the stage, etc. We bring the gift into form through our doing. We give shape to the creative impulse through action.

## FINDING THE BALANCE

As creators, we work with specific aspects of feminine and masculine energies each day in order to generate and sustain our lives, the realities we handcraft for ourselves choice by choice. Recognizing and understanding how to balance these energies accelerates our ability to create success in our own way.

Feminine energy is *generative*. It gives birth to manifestation, embodiment, expression . . . to all creativity. Masculine energy, on the other hand, is *sustaining*. It nurtures and preserves that which is created, supporting the continuation of all our creative efforts.

There are important exceptions, adding to the mystery. Love, for instance, is simultaneously a generative and sustaining energy, both a dynamic *doing* force and an animating power of *being*. Love creates art and meaning and worlds.

## The Generating Energies

The generating energies are feminine *being* energies. Wondrously, they *create* environments that foster ever more possibility. Think of one of your favorite creations, and you will see that it was generated out of one or more of the following states of being:

Willingness

Trust

Value

Joy

Appreciation

Care

Gratitude

Thankfulness

Expectation

Love

Contemplate these states for a moment. Although you can describe and express them, there is no *doing* inherently involved in them. When you are willing to truly experience these energies, your receptivity grows—and you become the beneficiary of the gift of creativity.

## *The Sustaining Energies*

The sustaining energies are the masculine *doing* energies. Giving form and shape, these are the energies of will and action that maintain and sustain a creative outcome once it has been generated.

You have probably had the experience of generating something you wanted, only to have it either quickly collapse or gradually fade away—a relationship, a friendship, a business, a brilliant idea. "I'm good at manifesting things," we might say. "I just can't seem to hang on to them." That is because it requires a very different set of energies to sustain something than it does to generate it.

The following are the primary sustaining energies:

Will

Discipline

Commitment

Ownership

Intimacy

Nurturance

Love

As sustaining energies, discipline and commitment go hand in hand. Discipline involves action steps that express a commitment through structure, principles, and consistency. This creates a powerful coherence or integrity. As creators, we also know the flip side of integrity, which shows up as obstruction. Many of the challenges presented by obstruction, in all its various guises, are challenges to discipline.

Ownership is a deep recognition and appreciation of our personal strengths and weaknesses, with responsibility and acceptance. It always requires that we tell ourselves the truth—*about ourselves*. Ownership can be uncomfortable for many because it does not—it cannot—deny power. For some, that can pass for ego or vanity. It is neither of those things. It is an active admission of power.

Intimacy, too, is active. To be close, tender, and vulnerable, and to increase trust, we must actively do something to meet the needs and preferences of the one we are caring for, whether that is another person or ourselves. In other words, we demonstrate our caring through our actions.

Surprisingly, although nurturance is typically thought of as a feminine quality, it is a masculine energy, an active cultivating, a *doingness* that coddles into form what has previously been formless.

## ACTIVITY AND POSSIBILITY— ANOTHER PERSPECTIVE

Another way to understand the sustaining energies is to consider the activities (the doing) involved in this book:

- making routines
- utilizing ritual
- inviting the muses
- embracing obstruction
- acting with courage in the face of that obstruction
- using practices and techniques with diligence
- expressing a commitment to yourself through each of these acts

All of these action steps are for the purpose of sustaining the outcomes and successes that you generate. This is your dance of creativity.

Another way to understand the generating energies is to consider them as the being states of *possibility*:

- the possibility of making routine
- the possibility of utilizing ritual
- the possibility of inviting the muses
- the possibility of embracing obstruction
- the possibility of possibility itself

All of these are being states that hold the possibility of creativity. They are states of being that are pregnant with potentials yet "unconceived."

## THE TEAMWORK OF WILL AND WILLINGNESS

One more way to understand both the differences and the harmonious interplay between the generating and sustaining energies is through the synergy of will and willingness.

The generating (feminine) energies have a quality of *willingness* as opposed to will. They are active but have no action steps. With generating energies we are not planning, building, carving, or otherwise making anything. We are in the *experience* of valuing, trusting, enjoying, caring, feeling grateful, or being excited. We are being.

In a sense, any adjective or noun we put "being" in front of can become a generating energy: being curious, being quiet, or even being a workaholic, since we have the ability to generate unpleasant experience, too.

From there, we flip to the sustaining (masculine) energies, where there is the *will* to "unpack" the gift of our experience. There is the will to live the life we have created for ourselves. Commitment, discipline, ownership, intimacy, and love are each enactments of the will that makes this possible.

Generating energies, like love and intimacy, are fully unleashed when they are expressed through the sustaining energies of will and action.

## THE WOMB OF CREATIVITY

Being states are the "womb" of creativity, where creative inspiration is planted as a seed within us. If we are at war with the feminine energies—the calamity of chauvinism—we preclude a relationship with the very source of our creative impulse and inspiration. As masculine and feminine qualities are often out of balance in our world, renewing intimacy with creativity means redressing the balance: more generating energies when needed, and more sustaining energies where needed.

Generating energies are encompassing energies. They surround and hold our creative potentials. The quality of our beingness establishes an environment that dictates the kind of thing we can create. It sets the temperature for what we are going to creatively "bake." At 400 degrees, we can make a cake, but we can't make ice cream. At 25 degrees, we can generate and sustain ice cream, but sorry, no pot roast.

When I am in a being state, the kind that expects struggle, then whatever it is that I create will be born through struggle. Likewise, in states of trust and wonder, whatever I create through my will and action will be imbued with qualities of trust and wonder.

Generating energies always involve an *openness* to value, joy, care, gratitude, and willingness. Sustaining energies always involve the *application* of will, intimacy, ownership, discipline, and love. In essence, the generating energies open the womb of creativity, and the sustaining energies fill it.

Steeped in the generating energies we are pregnant with creative potential. These feminine energies hold the boundaries of possibility that are filled by our doing, without regard to our gender. In the same way that a pregnant mother falls in love with her unborn child, we can find ourselves in love with what is yet unborn within us. This is the enchantment of the creative process.

> *In the same way that a pregnant mother falls in love with her unborn child, we can find ourselves in love with what is yet unborn within us.*

## A DAILY PRACTICE—IMAGINING POSSIBILITIES

This is a sustaining practice I do daily. It's a ritual for supercharging creativity and cultivating a relationship with generating energies. Throughout the day—when I wake up, when I go for walks, when I'm driving—I think about what I am joyful about: the friends I have, the love I have, the work I do. I focus on the generating energies of trust and appreciation. I allow myself to feel in my body how much trust I have in my wife and how much gratitude I feel for her presence in my life.

The radio in my car is broken, and I've purposely left it that way. I am appreciative of the time that gives me to feel and imagine. I make a practice of imagining different possibilities. I imagine myself in a world that is prosperous and abundant without getting bogged down in the reasons or "why nots." I see a world abundant in resources, solutions, opportunities, love, connection, and community.

The scenarios we envision don't have to be anchored in the realistic. That frees up imagination. You could imagine yourself on another planet if it helps your ability to stretch, to dream. On that planet you might see a sky, stars, and wildlife that you have never seen before. You can be free to creatively roam . . . to feel, experience, and be.

## Cultivating the Generating Energies

Choose times and places for imagining: before you get out of bed in the morning, during your commute to and from work, folding a basket of laundry, walking around your neighborhood, chopping vegetables, or any time you have to yourself. Then tune in to the generating energies:

- What and who do you trust?
- What and who do you value?
- What and who are you enjoying?
- What and who do you care about?
- What and who do you appreciate?
- What and who are you grateful for?

As you think about a creative project that you are currently engaged in or are planning to start, consider the following questions:

- What are your expectations in relationship to your project?
- Are you open and receptive to the experience of it?
- Beyond will and action, are you willing to engage in and commit to your project?

Write down the information that comes to you, or speak your answers into a recorder, which you can play back at a later time.

## BEYOND LOGIC AND REASON

Just as thoughts and feelings are always connected, generating and sustaining energies are always connected. If you tug at a thought long enough, you will come to a feeling, and vice versa. The same is true of generating and sustaining energies.

The creative magic is what bubbles up *between* the generating and sustaining energies, between the thought and feeling.

Sustaining energies exist inside of what is known and understood. We know and understand the world of action and activity very well. The generating energies, on the other hand, are beyond logic and reason. We usually talk about them in logical ways, attempting to explain *why* we feel joyful or trusting or filled with gratitude, etc. But when we do this, we are shoehorning those experiences to fit inside what we already know. We might say, "I'm joyful *because* _____ (because I spent time with people I love/because I got the promotion/because I won the award)." But the bigger relationship—the relationship between us and creativity—is discovered by understanding that those deeply felt experiences are larger than logic and reason alone can explain. It is the sustaining energies of will and action that bring these postlogical experiences into the realm of what is known.

We can look to some of our creative forebears to understand this interplay. Through his willingness to move beyond logic and reason, Picasso received a creative impulse that became an avant-garde art movement known as Cubism. He had an insight that arose from his imagination that he wanted to communicate so that others could experience it, too. He called on the sustaining energies of commitment and discipline to paint his inspired vision on the canvas. Prior to this time, human beings could not comprehend this nonlinear, deconstructed experience of reality. It was a new idea. Picasso found a way to express an idea that was bigger than the experience of the world, yet in a way that the world could experience it.

Like Picasso, Renaissance artists centuries earlier had conceived of a new way of conveying *perspective* and, with discipline, learned how to translate their experience of linear and atmospheric geometries in such a way that everyone could experience it. They introduced us to the "vanishing point" that is determined by a line in space.

Think back to the early 1990s and how we communicated in business and daily life. Remember the noisy gyrations of fax machines? Prior to the creation of email, the world looked and sounded one way. It is a very different world today.

Sourced beyond the realm of logic and reason, the generating energies are more dreamlike. The sustaining energies provide the focus, technique, craft, and discipline that allow us to take what is beyond logic and reason and give it form *inside* of logic and reason.

The net result: Together they expand the boundaries of what is logical and reasonable. They give us a map with a rolling frontier. That is how we move forward.

That is how we create.

## CHAPTER 14

# The Guardians of Ultracreativity: Paradox and Confusion

*It was a summer's day in winter*
*The rain was snowing fast*
*A little boy in snowshoes stood sitting on the grass*
—UNATTRIBUTED VERSE, "THE DYING FISHERMAN'S
SONG," AS TOLD BY MY DAD, ISAAC

While looking for a solution to a financial problem your company faced or working on the third chapter of your novel, did you ever wish you could tap into a geyser of creativity that flowed so effortlessly that you would never be bothered by a creative block again?

Because the world of structured imagining takes a straight-line approach to everything, we sometimes feel limited in our creative potentials and options. In order to get from Monday to Friday, we have to go through Wednesday. When we do decide to change the way things are (at work, at home, in our community, in our world), we are conditioned to refer to the past to determine the next logical step. In our imagination and dreams, however, we move by thought alone. We move efficiently and elegantly, unobstructed by a fixed blueprint of reality. As you develop your CQ—your creativity quotient—you are able to tap in to an entirely different paradigm. You enter the zone of ultracreativity. This is where infinite creativity exists and innovation begins. It is a reservoir from which you can draw anytime you want to.

To get there, you need to practice veering off the straight line.

## ULTRACREATIVITY—BEYOND THE STRAIGHT LINE

The mind balks when we try to consider what might lie beyond logic and reason. It goes nuts. "What use is THAT?" it cries. "What value is a creative pursuit if it has no apparent application—if I can't make money with it or fill a demand?"

"I have no idea" is the only honest response I can offer when my mind comes up with these objections. But here is what I do know: beyond logic and reason there is *more*.

At the frontier of reason, imagination does not stop. Control does.

Beyond structured imagining—shaped by the stories, beliefs, and values we have acquired from others—lies a dimension of imagination that *imagines itself*—the field from which every new idea and innovation is born.

From the lightbulb to the telephone to the World Wide Web, every single invention and every work of art that has ever been is not the result of a linear progression. Each one has arrived as a gift of imagining and spirit.

Remember Eros? When the dynamic qualities of will and action come together with the receptive qualities of imagining, feeling, and being, we invoke a great creative force. Eros sparks new thoughts, feelings, and relationships that bring flashes of intuition and genius. This merging of doing and being creates a field of possibilities.

This is ultracreativity.

By ourselves, we can do nothing. When we try to create in a vacuum, isolated and unassisted, we spend more time wrestling with our obstructions than we do innovating. But when we treat Eros with respect, ultracreativity flowers. We receive the gifts of inspiration and gain access to new dimensions of perceiving and conceiving.

How do we open to these possibilities? Is there a "trick" to loosening the grip of the logical mind? The trick is understanding *paradox* and *confusion*—the guardians of ultracreativity.

> *This merging of doing and being creates*
> *a field of possibilities. This is ultracreativity.*

## THE POWER OF PARADOX

We commonly think of paradox as something that exhibits a contradictory nature . . . and we tend to leave it at that. End of story. But paradox is much more than a contradiction.

Paradox is the holding of two or more separate frequencies of idea and/or action simultaneously without any loss of attention assets from either task. More important, it is *a channel of communication* through which our ultracreative selves reach out to us from beyond logic and reason.

## THE FUNCTION OF PARADOX— THE EXAMPLE OF BEAUTY

As the saying goes, beauty is in the eye of the beholder. We take in a sunset over the ocean, or Yosemite Valley in California, or a thoroughbred in the home stretch, and think, "Oh, my God, how beautiful."

The form a creation takes always follows its deeper *function*. Imagine that an architect is building your house. She asks, "How many people will you sleep? How much time will you spend in the kitchen or entertaining? Do you value being outdoors?" These functions will determine the form of your house: how many bedrooms, how many baths, the size of the dining room, the span of your patio, etc. This is an example of form following function.

Likewise, at the level of function, beauty itself holds a quality that both includes and transcends its appearance or form. It is always more than, and different from, the sum of its parts.

It is a paradox.

For those who are mathematically inclined, the equation looks like this:

*exhilaration + serenity / experienced simultaneously = beauty*

Beauty emerges when you experience the creative forces of exhilaration and serenity simultaneously. Thus beauty is the resolution of two paradoxical frequencies of creativity—exhilaration and serenity—lifting to a higher order of harmony and complexity. As our creativity quotient develops, not only can we more easily attune to the functions of paradox, *we can create with them.*

## INTENTIONALLY CULTIVATING PARADOX— FROM CONFUSION TO *CO-FUSION*

Imagine a funnel. Somewhere between the top and bottom of the funnel is a horizontal line. Above the line, we are unconscious. Below the line is conscious creativity. At the top of the funnel is the widest opening, the widest spectrum of creative potential, of reality creation itself.

As we descend below the line—passing through our structured imagining made of a collection of beliefs, attitudes, thoughts, feelings, and choices—our unlimited possibilities become reduced to probabilities.

We keep going down until we get to the bottom, the narrow end— the point where we produce creation.

Looking again from top to bottom, note that the top of the funnel is our broadest range of possibilities, a creative Niagara. The bottom end is what we actually create, a relative drop from a garden hose. At the narrow end, imagination and creativity are forces we seek to control. Outside the funnel and beyond it, these forces imagine WITH us.

As we become close to and familiar with paradox, we draw nearer to its mystery, moving from confusion to conscious *co-fusion.* Putting together two or more separate forces stretches the probability range of creative expression, as well as the possibility range of our creative potential. As this confluence of forces trickles down through the funnel, it expands the narrowest part, too.

At the level of *function*, we transmit the frequency we want to create. Although we know there will be an outcome, we don't know the *form* it will take because we are relinquishing control. We are doing our part and creativity is doing its part. If I'm a painter and I lay down a shade of red on a canvas, and then I lay down a shade of yellow over it and mix them, I have orange. When we approach thoughts, feelings, and emotions as an artist approaches his many paints—especially when mixing colors that might be considered opposing—we allow ourselves to be surprised by the merging of paradoxical elements, like serenity and exhilaration forming beauty.

## The Creativity Funnel

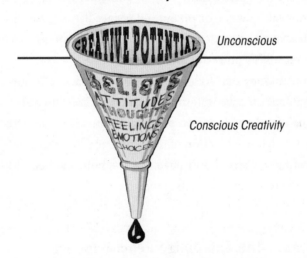

*Unconscious*

*Conscious Creativity*

## FAST-TRACKING CREATIVE INNOVATION

When you consciously play with paradox, holding two or more seemingly disparate things simultaneously, you are working with the fastest way to lay down the virgin brain connections that unleash ultra-creativity and innovation.

My dad used to recite a poem to me when I was little.
*It was a summer's day in winter*
*The rain was snowing fast*
*A little boy in snowshoes stood sitting on the grass*

I never tire of it. It is alive in my memory because it matters to me. Not only does it please me to remember my father this way, but it was the first time I experienced the creative exuberance that happens in the collision of unlike things. Called *amphigouri*, this type of enchanting, nonsensical writing or verse is an antidote to structured imagining because it does not communicate this or that, but something brand new that is between and unknown.

Creativity requires practice. Memory itself is a practice. Most often we engage memory unconsciously, rehashing the past for neurotic reasons, as when we don't wish to forget or forgive. Directing energy and focus in unhealthy ways, or on autopilot, is called a habit. For healthy reasons, it's called a practice. Either way, directing attention with intention is an incredibly powerful tool.

The techniques that follow will give you practice in intentionally turning on your creative waterfall. A heads-up: You will hear from your inner voice of judgment as you proceed, that critical voice that says, "I don't get it. What use is action with no practical applications?" Despite the protesting, go ahead and pave the way for new neural highways. Build them, and innovation will come.

## The Sharpened Pencil Practice

Close your eyes, and take a few slow, deep breaths.

STEP 1: Imagine yourself as a freshly sharpened yellow pencil, just like from your school days. You are standing on your finely sharpened lead point.

**STEP 2**: Imagine yourself slowly beginning to revolve on your pencil point, like a figure skater spinning on toe. First you are turning 45 degrees on point; continuing to 90 degrees; then 180 degrees. Keep going around and around, no stopping.

**STEP 3**: Keep going, spinning faster and faster—and yet faster still.

**STEP 4**: As you continue spinning without stopping, get ready to add another motion *at the same time.*

At the center point of the pencil that is you, start to imagine yourself tumbling from that center point, slowly at first, then faster and faster, end over end. You are spinning around and tumbling end over end at the same time. Spin and tumble. Continue for about thirty seconds.

**STEP 5**: Slow the tumble and slow the spin. Gently come back to your center and take a breath.

As you come to a gradual stop, notice any sensations, feelings, images, colors, thoughts, or ideas that might be arising. Jot down notes in your journal describing your experience.

If you were hooked up to a functional MRI or an EEG machine after concluding this visualization, your brain activity might look something like the fireworks on New Year's Eve or the Fourth of July.

## The Grace Note Practice

Close your eyes, and take a deep breath.

### First Tone

**STEP 1**: Imagine a musical tone. It can be one that is familiar—selecting from do, re, mi, fa, sol, la, ti—or any tone you hear in your imagination.

**STEP 2**: When you have this tone, imagine raising it. Progressing chromatically up your imaginative musical scale, raise it higher and higher. Keep going until you can no longer hear the tone. Even though you can't hear it, you know it is there. The human ear can hear as high as 20,000 hertz, as low as 20 hertz, and everything in between. The sound does not stop after 20,000 hertz, only our ability to connect to the sound.

**STEP 3**: Park this first tone, knowing it is there but currently raised beyond your ability to hear it.

### Second Tone

**STEP 4**: Imagine a second tone, different from the first tone. Once you have it, raise this tone as well. Lift it higher and higher up your imaginative scale until you can no longer hear it.

### Harmonic Third Tone—Your Grace Note

**STEP 5**: You now have two tones that you have imagined, both of which you have lifted beyond your hearing. These two tones are creative forces, and even though you cannot hear them, they exist. Together, they are creating a harmonic. When two tones are sounded, they create a third tone as a harmonic of both.

This tone is your personal *grace note*.

The two tones you began with, which you have lifted beyond your senses, created this third tone by themselves. The grace note does not need you to create it. And, like the first two, although you can't physically hear the harmonic tone of your grace note, you know it is there.

### Adding in Your Vision

**STEP 6**: Call up a vision of one of the things you most want to create for yourself, for another, or for our world. Imagine it. See it. Sense it. Feel it.

You can also think of this vision as a powerful form of prayer, because it largely bypasses your structured imagining.

**STEP 7**: Take your vision or prayer and imagine attaching it to, or laying it on, your grace note. Allow your grace note to lift it up and float away into the universe.

Take a breath and come back to center.

Now in the presence of this vision, let's take it even further.

## The Ultrasight Practice

Find your comfortable place to relax, breathe, and become still.

**STEP 1**: Begin by looking straight ahead with your eyes open but also relaxed.

**STEP 2**: Close your eyes and imagine that your ability to see is boundless. With your awareness, lift up your eyes and look straight out through the top of your head.

**STEP 3**: Dropping down slightly, imagine that your eyes are moving back 90 degrees, until you are looking straight at the back of your head.

**STEP 4**: Imagine that your eyes are shifting down another 90 degrees, and you are looking straight down your spinal cord.

**STEP 5**: Invoke a vision of something you want to create for yourself, for another, or for your world. This vision can be one that you have already summoned or something new. It can be a creative project geared toward business, art, community, your relationship—whatever you are inspired to create and share.

**STEP 6**: Imagine that you have placed this vision on your eyes, and look straight down your spinal cord again.

STEP 7: Like pulling back on the bar of a spring-loaded mousetrap and quickly releasing it, feel the rush of energy as your eyes snap back into their normal position, catapulting your vision into the universe—into the realm of Ultracreativity.

Come back to center. Take a breath. And open your physical eyes.

The next exercise is a practice in conscious *co-fusion*. You will put together two separate things, both of which should have great meaning for you. While this technique might be challenging at first, trust the process. Even when it feels uncomfortable, it will show you that the mother lode of your creative power can be mined in the space between your thoughts and feelings. The positive impact of creating with this technique can be far-reaching.

## The Space-Between Practice

Get comfortable and close your eyes.

STEP 1: Behind the screen of your closed lids, imagine your most joyful future; imagine your heart's desire with respect to whatever it is you want to create for yourself, for another, or for your world. Feel it, sense it, and see it as best you can. It doesn't have to be a perfect connection. Feeling it is the key.

STEP 2: Move your joyful future over to the right-hand side of the inner screen behind your eyes.

STEP 3: Imagine your worst terror, your darkest fear, your most frightening thought. A few examples: "I will get sick and be a burden." "I will lose my partner." "I will be living out of a shopping cart under a bridge." Whatever it is, do not be afraid to see it and feel it.

**STEP 4:** Move that image and experience to the left-hand side of the screen behind your eyes.

**STEP 5:** On your inner screen, you now have your heart's desire on your right side and your worst nightmare on your left side. Your visualization of them doesn't have to be in vivid detail; just feel them as best you can.

**STEP 6:** Imagine yourself stepping into the middle of the two scenarios, into the space between your most joyful future and your worst nightmare. Experience yourself in the field right between these two potentials. Spend as much time here as you feel comfortable, which can be as brief as two or three minutes.

Come back to center, take a breath, and let it all go.

Facing your darkest fear releases the creative energy that is bound up in a web of hidden anxieties. You are dissipating its power. Now your attention and imagination can go to work creating brilliant futures. You can also benefit from using this practice when fear and anxiety aren't so hidden.

During the global financial crisis of 2008, we lost all our savings. The only thing that kept me sane was the Space-Between Practice. It allowed me to respond creatively to the challenges of that time with insight and innovation. I found new ways to move forward and the wherewithal to keep trusting.

Let go of any worry about which future awaits you. It is your willingness to do the exercise that casts the vote between potentials. Even if it's a fifty-fifty split, *your willingness itself is the creative factor*—your willingness to be the creator, large enough to hold both possibilities.

You have just demonstrated for yourself the power of paradox. Use the above exercises again and again to advance your creative capacities.

# *Try This!*

## BECOMING A PRODIGY OF PARADOX— A QUICK-START PRACTICE

Practice suggestions: for use while driving, riding an elevator, on a bus, in the shower, or any environment where you have a few minutes for imagining.

- Settle down, close your eyes if appropriate, and imagine the velvety warmth of a horse's muzzle.
- At the same time, imagine fingernails clawing down a blackboard.
- What is your felt experience of each scenario? Is it exuberance and a warm feeling in your heart along with shivers? Is it comfort with irritation? Whatever your perceptions, hold both experiences simultaneously.

Play with this from time to time, summoning other opposites and experiencing them simultaneously. Each time you practice, you will be laying down virgin neuronal patterns that will find ways to be creatively expressed. Very quickly, you will become a virtuoso of this new practice—playing with paradox.

## CHAPTER 15

# *The Uncommon Senses: Rediscovering Intuition*

*There is no logical way to the discovery of these elemental laws.*
*There is only the way of intuition, which is helped by a feeling*
*for the order lying behind the appearance.*
**—ALBERT EINSTEIN**

What guides your creative choices? In addition to your values, what signals do you pick up on that spark your creativity and prompt you to take action? Have you ever said, "I had a feeling, and I just had to act on it"? Or, "I don't know where it came from, but in a flash I saw what I needed to do next"? What inner perceptions are you responding to in these moments?

In his book *The Second Brain*, Dr. Michael Gershon, chairman of the Department of Anatomy and Cell Biology at New York–Presbyterian Hospital/Columbia University Medical Center, wrote that there are more than 100 million neurotransmitters in the gut, which is approximately the same number found in the brain. Additionally, nearly every chemical that controls the brain, including various hormones, has also been identified in the gut. This explains why we get butterflies before a speech, a performance, or a big meeting or an upset stomach before a test. Through the work of the Institute of HeartMath we know there are neurons in the heart as well.

New research continues to reveal fascinating data regarding the vast network of communication taking place within the human body, which points to the neurological basis of one of our most essential creative faculties: *intuition*.

## INTUITION—ULTRACREATIVE COMMUNICATION

Intuition doesn't reside in the head. An acting teacher told me long ago that the entire body is a map of the subconscious mind—our great creative ally. I believe it. Beyond our mental capacities alone, beyond structured imagining, we are continuously in communication with the world inside and around us. In relationship with what is visible, as well as what is unseen, we continuously send and receive messages at the invisible level of energy or frequency. This powerful form of communication is our intuition at work.

But what is this intuition, really?

## DISCOVERING THE UNCOMMON SENSES— FACULTIES OF INTUITION

Everybody has experienced uncommon sensing. We call it intuition. Musicians find the groove and CEOs pay attention to hunches. Our creative instincts and feelings operate alongside the common senses on which we rely for calibrating physical reality—sight, smell, taste, hearing, and touch. However, we also have *uncommon senses* that contribute to the "gut feelings" that spark all our creative choices. These uncommon senses calibrate nonphysical reality, meaning everything that is beyond sight, smell, taste, hearing, and touch. Most of us would agree that there is more to us than we are able to experience with our physical senses alone. The uncommon senses include subtleties of perception: warmth, movement, presence, light, and substance that you may find stirringly or strangely familiar.

### Warmth

We already understand warmth as it relates to temperature. A sunny day in the springtime, or the air around a bonfire. But there is also

152

emotional warmth—the warmth of friends and strangers, the warmth of the heart that creates feelings of connection. As a felt-sense in the body, this heart-fueled warmth is experienced as aliveness. It is an energetic exuberance.

## Movement

Commonly understood relative to speed and motion, there are also movements that relate to *flow*. Creative flow, the flow of one's growth, even the flow of consciousness—especially that which streams forth when passion is fired up. In this sense, movement refers to the emotional progression of things that touch our hearts. To a creator, flow is a sensitivity to the *soul movement* of things. It is the subtle current tracing the inevitable progression toward greater love and freedom.

> *Flow is the subtle current tracing the inevitable progression toward greater love and freedom.*

## Presence

Presence is the "it factor" that we often assign to celebrities, but it is something we all have. It is the sum of our image, self-love, and self-respect.

*Charisma* and *voice* both point to this same signature quality we call presence. When we refer to someone having charisma, we typically imagine a larger-than-life persona, but this does not capture the true nature of charisma. It is a quality that refers to the unique impact of our presence. A creator asks, "What is my impact on you? And what is your impact on me?" As we ask these questions with more and more regularity, it becomes second nature. We become more conscious of the intricacies of impact, and all our relationships benefit from that growing awareness. Eventually, it becomes first nature. Presence becomes a practice.

Although we often think of voice as the particular tonal qualities that we hear when someone speaks, there are subtler frequencies to voice. Intimately linked to charisma, there is a distinctive quality of communication that speaks through the heart, also imparting a unique impact on others. Each of us has a subtle signature that is our presence, yet we tend to mimic others until we mature into the discovery of our own voice and charisma. When we come to understand our presence, we are able to see others more clearly as well. Being truly seen is a gift that creates a presence of its own, which the one being seen can feel, too.

## Light

Another uncommon sense is light. One aspect of light is the *radiance* that many people and places emanate. Imagine a sunset, a majestic landscape, or the face of a child or dear friend. As we learn to detect the light in others and in the things around us, we also discover luminous variations of the light within us. With its reflective abilities, radiance mirrors back that which is good and true. In this sense, radiance is a spiritual brilliance that reveals our connection with the unseen. Saints depicted in the works of the artistic masters are portrayed with halos and surrounded by a luminosity, all of which is a reference to this radiance.

Light also refers to an emotional *levity*. Woven into our body, mind, and spirit as an emotional quality, levity is an attitude of being that can include humor—the kind of humor that seeks to uplift by revealing truth, as opposed to humor that is cynical, nihilistic, and comes at the expense of oneself or others. Like radiance, levity is a quality of spiritual brilliance that provides a window of connection with the unseen. It arises naturally as we learn compassion for others and ourselves.

## Substance

The last of the uncommon senses is substance. Beyond "matter" in the physical domain, there is a sense of what *matters*—what matters emotionally, physically, mentally, and spiritually. As creators, we can actively look for the significance of things and for what matters to us, especially at the level of impact. For example, in relationship with the other uncommon senses, substance leads us to ask life-affirming questions, such as, "What impact do I want to have on others? What impact do I want them to have on me? What moves their hearts to excitement? What ignites the passions and stirs the souls of others?" The answers are fuel for the creative life.

## SUMMONING THE UNCOMMON SENSES

When you tap into any one of the uncommon senses, you are developing intuition. Begin to distinguish the uncommon senses, start paying attention to them. Experiment. Explore.

Study the light shining through people and things. Sense the movement in others related to their growth and the expansion of their awareness. Sense the warmth in others or the lack of it. You can even do this while watching television: sense the warmth or the lack of it coming from the program you're watching; sense its substance and how it might correlate with what matters to you.

The following exercise will give you a starting point and a set of prompts for recognizing the uncommon senses. The more that you actively seek them, the more they will make themselves known to you.

### Intuitive Sensing—Practicing the Uncommon Senses

Find a comfortable place to relax and write. Take ten to fifteen minutes for this meditative journaling exercise.

**STEP 1:** Bring into your awareness someone you love. This is someone you are close to, someone you enjoy being with, someone who inspires you.

**STEP 2:** Invoking your ordinary or common senses, see this person's face, hear the sound of their voice, and remember how it feels to touch their hand or to put your arms around them.

**STEP 3**: Begin to sense your loved one through the uncommon senses. Without straining to "get it right," give yourself permission to write down the first words and images that come to mind:

*Warmth.* Describe the emotional warmth of this person. How is it transmitted or expressed? How do you experience their warmth?

_____

_____

_____

_____

_____

*Movement.* Sense the soul movement taking place within this person. For example, is there some type of creative expression or emotional expression that makes this flow evident? How is their passion expressed?

_____

_____

_____

_____

_____

*Presence.* Sense the presence of this person, the potency of their image, self-love, and self-respect. Sense the charisma and voice that expresses the unique signature of their presence. With their presence in mind, describe their impact on you.

_____

_____

_____

_____

_____

*Light.* Sense the light emanating from this person. How do you experience this light? Is it a radiance that reflects back to you what is good and true and brilliant about you? Do they uplift through humor, expressing an emotional levity—a levity that is born of compassion? Do they radiate a spiritual brilliance that reminds you of your connection with the divine?

_____

_____

_____

_____

_____

**Substance.** Imagine this person in front of you one more time, sensing their substance. What matters to them, what has significance for them emotionally, physically, mentally, and spiritually? Describe one of the ways you experience their substance, whether it is something they do, something they create, or a quality of being they express.

_____

_____

_____

_____

_____

_____

_____

In this exercise, the qualities you have observed in the person you love also provide a mirror. What do you see reflected back at you? Do you recognize the light, warmth, movement, presence, and substance of *you*?

# CHAPTER 16

# *The Five Creative Talents*

*We live in the world when we love it.*
—RABINDRANATH TAGORE

As human beings, we are heir to talents that are integral to the creative life. We strengthen and refine these aptitudes every time we approach our lives as works of art. We could also refer to these talents as capacities for success.

The five creative talents are:

- Living
- Loving
- Leaving
- Learning
- Laughing

As with the other forces of creativity we have explored, the five talents are powerful energies that can lift us to the higher octave of ultracreativity. As we embrace the complexities of living and loving, becoming more and more intimate with our lives, we open the channels of communication with imagination, inspiration, and innovation.

## LIVING

The first talent is living. What is it to really live? To be engaged and involved? To be committed to participating fully? I look to our movie action heroes as reminders of what it is to make a talent of creative living.

- They show up, participating at full throttle.
- They are visible.
- They are adventurous.
- They take calculated risks.
- They enjoy life—working hard, eating well, and celebrating often.
- They are aware of the balance of being in the world but not of it.
- They do not see themselves as victims. They are the prime movers in the unfolding story. They are agents of change.
- They take upon themselves the responsibility of the world, *responding* to the challenges of life. They don't wait for others. They don't blame. They don't make excuses. *No true action hero has ever made an excuse.*

The nineteenth-century French writer Émile Zola articulated the credo of every worthy action hero and every creator, saying, "If you ask me what I came to do in this world, I, an artist, will answer you: I am here to live out loud."

For me, a creative life means that I actively reach out to meet the world. I allow myself to have impact in the world, and I allow myself to be affected *by* the world. I allow others to feel the consequences of my being alive and vice versa. I fully enjoy what life has to offer, with my senses awake and alive. In addition to my five senses, I explore the uncommon senses, including warmth, light, and substance. As much as possible, I am not in denial of my thoughts and feelings. I am an explorer of all the boundaries that are possible for me to enjoy.

The essence of creative living is the capacity to give and receive, both being necessary to participate fully in life.

Back to the action hero and the all-in way they live: we won't support a hero in our movies who offers anything less, and I am certain that I don't want to accept less from myself in my own life.

> *The essence of creative living is
> the capacity to give and receive.*

## LOVING

Loving is a talent to be cultivated over a lifetime. As both a generating and a sustaining energy, loving is a commitment we make to ourselves and to others. *It is also a relationship with every process of creativity that matters in our lives.*

To develop an artistry of love means . . .

- to give and to receive with an open heart
- to create safety for the self and others
- to reduce fear for self and others, including the fear of humiliation and the fear of abandonment
- to suspend negating judgments
- to give physical, emotional, mental, and spiritual appreciation and gratitude
- to provide pleasure as and where it is appropriate
- to honor
- to value
- to give dignity

As you contemplate these expressions of love, notice how they apply to creative pursuits. Do you bring to your work, your projects, or your art a sense of pleasure, valuing, and celebration?

Encourage your creative processes by reducing criticism and minimizing fears of rejection, humiliation, and failure, both for yourself and others. For example, whether you are writing a business plan, a book, or a symphony, one way to be loving with yourself is to be mindful of your self-talk. What are you saying to yourself about your abilities, your methods, your timing, or results? In every creative process and act, it is love that gives the object of our attention dignity.

Regardless of how much we love our line of work or the businesses we've built, we know that they aren't capable of loving us back. A consulting firm is not loving us back. A screenplay is not loving us back. A painting is not loving us back. Yet our creations do give us a sense of value. They provide us an experience of union and communion with mysterious cocreative forces, and as a result we are changed. By being so changed, we honor them.

In the weeks before *What Dreams May Come*, a love story that takes place in the afterlife, opened in theaters, our trailers were in heavy rotation on national television and caught the eye of a young teen whose name was Amanda. The subject held a special significance for Amanda, who was in the hospital at the end stage of a long terminal illness. My partner and I received a call from her dad, who told us that Amanda had seen an ad on TV and had become intent on seeing the movie. She told her parents that she wouldn't be alive when the movie came out, but she needed to see it somehow. He also shared with us that Amanda was very afraid of dying, and that they wanted to help her in every way possible to find comfort and a sense of safety.

We immediately arranged for the film to be shown in her hospital room, but didn't hear anything back for some time.

When Amanda's father called again, he described how her family and friends had gathered together at her bedside to watch the movie. Afterward she expressed how much less afraid she felt, and she passed away soon after.

A movie, a postcard, or a soufflé. Our creations have impact, and as a result, their effects can change us.

## LEAVING

The talent of leaving has two distinct layers of meaning. The first layer has to do with what are we prepared to move beyond; it is an opportunity to learn how to let go. The second relates to what we are leaving behind—the maps we are making to ease the way for ourselves and others.

In this way, it is important to see yourself honestly, so that you can recognize any patterns and behaviors that hold you back. Then draw on your discipline, a sustaining energy, to cut those patterns loose and let them go. Is there a relationship, a project, a job, a lifestyle habit that you need to release? By cultivating the talent of leaving, you can become like the master gardener who knows that before he plants a new crop, the cuttings of the old one need to be turned under. The book of Ecclesiastes gives this perennial reminder of the importance of leaving: "To every thing there is a season, and a time to every purpose under the heaven . . . a time to plant, and a time to pluck up that which is planted . . ."

As you practice leaving as a creative talent, surprises unfold. You become more concerned with where you are going than where you have been. You free yourself to make extraordinary steps forward. Mohandas Gandhi was doing very well as a lawyer, yet there came a point when he made the decision to leave his vocation for *the more* that was possible. Inspiring civil rights movements across the world, he became Mahatma Gandhi—*Mahatma* being the Sanskrit word for "Great Soul." In the expression of his art, Picasso decided to leave behind the methods he knew for what he did not yet know.

In my personal life, I frequently take stock: *What can I leave behind so that I can be more creatively productive going forward? What can I release that will free me up to bring greater creative resources to others and the world?*

## THE MAPS YOU ARE LEAVING BEHIND

The other kind of leaving has to do with the maps we leave behind for others—guides and resources for living, growing, and evolving. Sometimes this is talked about as legacy. Ask yourself, "What maps have I made to ease the way? What maps am I making right now that support others to be more and to live more?"

Tucked inside the talent of leaving is a secret: there are no passive observers in the universe; there are only creators.

Participation and contribution is everything.

Many years ago my family was vacationing in Italy. On the way home we passed through Rome at the same time that the World Youth Day was underway. The entire city was overflowing with pilgrims, food, music, and dance. It was a beautiful sight. I noticed everyone carrying large gift bags—"swag bags" bursting at the seams. Just as I said to my wife, "I wonder what's in those gift bags?" I heard my daughter's voice rise above the din. "Hey, there's *Daddy*!" she proclaimed. She had spotted the cover of *The Jesus Film*, the first movie I worked on right out of college in the late 1970s. Although the *New York Times* has described it as the most-watched motion picture of all time, working on it as a young writer felt like lifetimes ago. Now here we were in the streets of Rome, and the Vatican was giving it away in countless languages to thousands of young people.

> *There are no passive observers in the universe.*
> *There are only creators.*
> *Participation and contribution is everything.*

## LEARNING

Learning is another talent that we will continue to hone and refine for a lifetime. Doing this requires that we take stock of what we have learned over the course of our lives so far:

- What tools of creativity have I acquired?
- What creative skills have I learned and developed?
- What insights and skills have I acquired emotionally, physically, and mentally?
- How have I equipped myself to deal creatively with my relationships—with my spouse or partner, children, friends, colleagues, mentors, employers, etc.?
- How have I equipped myself to deal creatively with myself, including my past and my future selves?
- How have I equipped myself to deal creatively with the uncertainty and mystery?

Reviewing what we have learned up to this point is a step toward owning those tools and skills, but not for proclaiming that we have the rules of the game down pat, i.e., "I've learned everything I need to know, and now I'm done" or "I know how life works. I've finally figured it all out."

As a creative talent, learning is intimately connected to *humility*. If humility were given a voice, it would say, "Even though I understand the world in one way, in the very next instant, I can know it in an entirely different way. In the very next instant, my whole world can change."

I was fifteen years old the first time I experienced Stanley Kubrick's film *2001: A Space Odyssey*. My whole world turned upside down. I learned that there were possibilities beyond my teenaged imaginings.

At the heart of humility is an open-mindedness and openhearted-ness with an inexhaustible appetite for illumination.

## LAUGHING

The fifth creative talent is the power to laugh, to lighten up about life, and to celebrate it, no matter what we have gone through. "This too will pass" is a powerful attitude to cultivate and practice. It can be augmented by asking yourself the following questions:

- Do I take myself too seriously, or can I shrug off my shortcomings?
- Do I take my creativity too seriously, or can I allow myself to make mistakes?
- Can I own the desperate dance that I sometimes do for belonging, for meaning, for connection?
- Can I take with a grain of salt all the ways in which I struggle for love when I have been loved all along?
- All in all, can I see the humor in life?

Laughter really is the best medicine. In the early 1980s, journalist Norman Cousins wrote *Anatomy of an Illness,* a book that spent forty weeks on the *New York Times* bestseller list. Emphasizing the healing neurochemistry of laughter, it broke new ground, encouraging patients to partner with their doctors in the process of reclaiming their health. Cousins's story of laughing his way from illness to health is one of the best-known cases in the field of study now known as psychoneuroimmunology, which examines how what we think affects the brain, leading to changes in the immune system. When you have a good laugh, when you are able to rise up from the mire of seriousness and worry, the changes are often immediate. You take in more oxygen, blood circulation increases, blood pressure typically drops, and muscles begin to relax. This cascade effect includes the proliferation of white blood cells for fighting infection, the release of endorphins, our natural pain-relievers, as well as a decrease in cortisol and epinephrine, the stress hormones.

Bottom line: When you are delighted, your whole body is delighted. When you feel connected to yourself in moments of spontaneous outbursts of joy, you feel more connected to others as well. We could easily call the surges of creative inspiration that often accompany moments of humor, lightness, and connection "the neurochemistry of creativity."

## The Five Talents—A Journaling Process

Set aside thirty minutes for this exercise. Find an inspiring place to work where the muses can come sit with you, such as your desk with a cup of coffee or under a tree at your favorite park.

### PART I—Assessing the Five Creative Talents
### *Living*

In what part of my life am I holding back, not showing up fully, and afraid to take risks? Is there an area of my life where I see myself as a victim rather than an agent of change?

_____

_____

_____

_____

_____

_____

_____

_____

In what parts of my life am I already reaching out to others and the world? In what ways am I participating fully in life?

_____

_____

_____

_____

_____

_____

_____

## *Loving*

Is there an area of my life where I'm not giving enough? In what ways can I be open to receiving more? *Who* could I honor by allowing them to change me? And *what* could I honor by allowing it to change me?

_____

_____

_____

_____

_____

_____

_____

How do I create safety for myself and others? In what ways do I reduce fear and increase pleasure for myself and others?

_____
_____
_____
_____
_____
_____
_____

### Leaving

What am I ready and willing to let go of in order to grow and evolve? What is it time to move beyond, and am I prepared to do that?

_____
_____
_____
_____
_____
_____
_____

What are the maps that I'm leaving in the world, both for the benefit of myself and others?

_____
_____
_____
_____
_____
_____
_____

### Learning

What are the tools, skills, and insights I have acquired that I get the most pleasure and fulfillment from employing? Are there tools and skills gathering dust that I would benefit from putting to use?

_____

_____

_____

_____

_____

_____

_____

_____

What situation or circumstance in my life is inviting me to approach it with humility? In what part of my life could I be more open to change and possibility?

_____

_____

_____

_____

_____

_____

_____

_____

### Laughing

What am I taking too seriously in my life right now? What situation, challenge, or habit am I keeping locked in place with the weight of worry, fear, or judgment?

_____

_____

_____

_____

_____

_____

_____

_____

What aspects of myself and my life do I approach with humor and awareness?

_____

_____

_____

_____

_____

_____

_____

## PART II—Being Discovered by the Five Creative Talents

What does the talent of **Living** want me understand at this moment in my life? What does it want me to know about commitment, participation, visibility, risk, or enjoyment?

_____

_____

_____

_____

_____

_____

What does the talent of **Loving** want me to know right now? How can I create safety for another? Or what can I give emotionally, physically, or spiritually that will be an expression of my loving?

_____

_____

_____

_____

_____

_____

_____

What does the talent of **Leaving** most want me to understand or feel? Is it giving me the strength and trust to let go of an old way of being? Or is it reminding me to fully share my gifts with this world?

_____

_____

_____

_____

_____

_____

_____

What does the talent of **Learning** want me to know about humility—about the willingness to be changed and being open to new possibilities?

_____

_____

_____

_____

_____

_____

_____

What does the talent of **Laughing** want me to know? What does it want me to feel? What does it have to tell me about lightness, humor, and celebration?

_____

_____

_____

_____

_____

_____

_____

_____

## CHAPTER 17

# *Your Real Work:*
# *Where Personal Innovation*
# *Meets Purpose*

*One must still have chaos in oneself to be*
*able to give birth to a dancing star.*
—FRIEDRICH NIETZSCHE

While we are always creating—every minute of every day—many of us seem to have little time or energy to innovate. When we cling to the familiarity of structured imagining, we hold innovation at bay. If we give ourselves some creative breathing room, it can arrive—in the form of new sales and marketing strategies for our businesses, new stories for our movies and books, new ways of enlivening our classrooms, new ways to demonstrate the love we have for our partner or children. The possibilities are endless.

When the dynamism of *doing* comes together with the receptivity of *being*, creative innovation cannot be stopped. We sense the pulsing of new life stirring our thoughts and feelings. We sense the call of what is yet unborn.

Innovation is about setting out to cross a river, but not just any river—a river so broad that you can't see across to the other side. This requires trust and optimism because you are building a bridge in front of you as you go.

## SPRINTING FORWARD

A powerful example of innovation in business can serve as personal inspiration when we can't see what lies ahead. In the late 1970s, Southern Pacific Railroad had 15,000 miles of uninterrupted rail bed and decided to lay digital networking cables along all their tracks. At that time, the Bell system had a total telecommunications monopoly, so laying this cable made zero sense. There seemed to be no end to Bell's domination. Even so, someone in charge realized that they had this highly valuable, interconnected real estate tying together across the whole country and acted on it. Then the day came when the government deregulated the entire telephone industry, and years ahead of everyone else, the railroad had already created the basis for a nationwide fiber optic network. Today, Southern Pacific Railroad is history, but *Southern Pacific Railroad Internal Network Telecommunications*, otherwise known as SPRINT, carries on.

This story illustrates the point that, if we build it, they will come. If we innovate, supporting circumstances will come. The road will always rise to meet us. That is ultracreativity.

What do you want to build? And do you trust that support, opportunity, and possibility will be there for you?

Maybe the most important question is, are you willing to cross the river of innovation in the pursuit of your dreams without a guarantee as to what is on the other side?

## KNOWING WITHOUT CERTAINTY— A KEY TO PERSONAL INNOVATION

Exploring ultracreativity is a practice that opens us. Paradoxically, it opens us to knowing, but it is a knowing *without* certainty—a knowing where the heart leads the way. The author Wendell Berry understood this well:

*It may be that when we no longer know what to do*
*we have come to our real work,*

*and that when we no longer know which way to go*
*we have come to our real journey.*

*The mind that is not baffled is not employed.*
*The impeded stream is the one that sings.*

No matter what has come before—no matter how many successes and failures you have under your belt, you can innovate right where you are. Personal innovation is taking action toward something beyond the points of reference of your past experiences and memories but without losing sight of your past experiences and memories. The point of connection between the two is where you will meet your real work.

## SIGNALS, CLUES, AND CLARITY

"There is one thing in this world that must never be forgotten." With that, the poet Rumi urged us to remember our real work. Trusting that everyone comes into this world with a particular task and purpose, he was telling us that *why* we do what we do is more significant than *what* we do. And by remembering our infinite presence, we become clear about our "why." We become increasingly skillful at choosing where to put our attention and energy when we are conscious of the feelings we seek to experience, as with The Most Amazing Thing. Our purpose and mission become clearer when we understand the dance of *being* and *doing* that is always taking place within us.

Regardless of your age, education, or professional experience, you will be called to your real work. That call will never cease. It is a summoning from the soul that cannot be quelled. I know many extraordinary people who have retired from their former careers and are deeply and actively committed to their real work. *And they have no intention of giving that up, ever.*

If you aren't clear right now about your real work, look for the clues and signals that life is putting in front of you. Your gifts, talents, strengths, and values are all pointing to it. Your desires, passions, and dreams are pointing to it as well.

And yes, The Most Amazing Thing also points to your real work. Notice that it's not "The Most Okay Thing" or "The Most Widely Acceptable Thing." It's the most AMAZING thing because it brings you more alive.

In the same way, your real work inspires you. It lifts you, and therefore it's uplifting to those who are affected *by* you.

Sometimes, finding your real work begins with discovering what it is *not*. For example, I know that I am not my job. My job descriptions are canvases: husband, father, author, producer. I depend on them to work out what's important to me through the driving *whys* of my creativity. Yet somewhere, deep under my layer cake of whys, I know that I matter. I care. The deep root has juice. So I commit to deepening my relationship and love affair with the world. That is my real work.

If you are in search of your real work, the following questions can put you on the trail:

*What do you want to express?*

*What do you care about?*

*What do you love?*

*What do you want to give?*

If you are already on the trail of your real work—in touch with your creative fire and passions—it is important to express it and act on it with courage and commitment.

Not long ago, I co-led a workshop for a team at an oil company in Canada. It was a tough room at first, especially so because the head of HR was skeptical about the value of a conversation about creativity. *What does creativity have to do with the oil business?*, he challenged. Responding to that signal, I decided to make a slight but important adjustment, starting off the day by leading a talk about the people, experiences, and places that stimulated the team's passions. *I'm passionate about extreme sports, travel, gardening, investing, guitar playing, my grandchildren, my classroom, the environment*—all were typical responses, yet none of these things *are* passion. They are merely outlets for it.

The *aliveness* that is experienced and expressed in the pursuit of those things: that is passion. And there are many ways to discover it.

Despite his apprehension, the head of HR was a good sport and participated in an exercise to tap into his passion. On day two of the workshop, he surprised us all with uncharacteristic vulnerability. He reported that he had shared his workshop experience with his wife the previous evening. He looked years younger as he spoke with candor about the romantic fire that was awakened after long years of lying dormant.

This corporate executive had kindled Eros, the passionate quality underlying all creativity—a presence and focus that is so intense that we can lose track of time.

Eros can be awakened for *everything*, not just sex. It is a creative principle, as we discussed in the earlier chapters about the feminine and masculine principles of being and doing. But there is so little room for it in modern life that we resort to sexualizing things as our last hope for tapping its enormous power. It doesn't have to be that way. We each have the ability to light the fires of passion at will, directing eros to every aspect of our lives, from the most mundane to the most sublime. It is the birthright of a creative life.

As for the HR director, he was so moved that he wrote a letter asking what it would take to come work with me and deepen his connection with creativity. Underneath his initial resistance was a great hunger for aliveness. Less than a year after the workshop, he left the oil company, and he is now pursuing his real work with passion. He received certification as an executive coach and is building a thriving practice of his own design.

> *That call of your real work will never cease.*
> *It is a summoning from the soul that cannot be quelled.*

## Your Creative Mission—A Four-Step Process

Close your eyes and take a few deep breaths. Sense the connection you have with your creative self in preparation for the following steps.

**STEP 1**: What do you desire to birth into the world? What is your creative mission? Your favorite form of creative expression? Let a picture come together. If you are on the search for your real work, just imagine for a moment that you *do* know, or ask your future self to give you an advance screening.

**STEP 2**: Put this picture into words. Write a paragraph describing your creative mission in detail. How is your mission connected to your purpose? Describe the passion that fuels your desire to create, to give, and to express yourself. If you are unsure, use this exercise as a stream of consciousness device. Allow your creative imagination to take you where your structured imagining hasn't dared to go.

_____

_____

_____

_____

_____

_____

_____

_____

_____

_____

_____

_____

_____

**STEP 3**: Using the Vocabulary of Feelings list in Chapter 4 (page 36), scan for the empowered adjectives that correlate with your purpose and passion. Pick five to ten words. Examples: *contented, ecstatic, elated, euphoric, relaxed, worthy,* or others that resonate for you. If words come to you that aren't on the list, that's good, too. The important thing is that the words feel uplifting to you.

_____

_____

_____

_____

_____

**STEP 4**: Read your creative mission out loud in the voice of each uplifting quality and frequency. If *confident* is one of your words, read your mission with the voice of confidence. If *serene* is one of your words, read your mission with the voice of serenity, etc.

To complete, take a few minutes to write about your experience of speaking with the voice of each empowering quality. Are there certain thoughts, feelings, or sensations that stand out for you?

If you weren't completely comfortable reading your creative mission out loud in the different voices, you are not alone. But I assure you, this exercise is worth the stretch. With practice, and within a short amount of time, you will embody these qualities. They will be the prism through which your creativity is vividly expressed.

## BECOMING REAL

The road to discovering your creative mission, your real work, isn't always a walk in the park—but it is a journey that can lead you home to who you really are.

Just ask the bullfighter.

Looking directly into the fearsome face of the creature not more than four feet in front of him, El Pilar, as he was known, tugged on the waistcoat of his "suit of lights"—the ornate costume he wore each time he entered the arena. With sweat stinging his eyes, he swallowed hard to suppress the thought that loomed larger than the beast whose hot breath struck him every few seconds. The rhythm of their breathing now synchronized, the *torero* looked into the dark and luminous eyes of the bull, and he just knew.

It was over.

The kill would not happen—not now, not ever again.

Álvaro Múnera Builes was a celebrated bullfighter from Colombia, South America, who had fought and performed his way to Spain—and into the hearts of fans throughout the Latin world. He had achieved the fame, riches, and adulation that many know as wistful fantasy.

Although Builes had stood nose to nose with the bulls a thousand times before, this time he would walk away. Much to the shock and bewilderment of the mass of onlookers, he surrendered his cape right there and then, abdicating his rock star status and all that came with it.

His compassion had grown larger than his lust for glory.

As the story goes, when Builes came out of seclusion weeks later, he spoke about the realization he had that day in the dust of the stadium: "Suddenly, I looked at the bull. He had this innocence that all animals have in their eyes, and he looked at me with this pleading. It was like a cry for justice, deep down inside of me. I describe it as being like a prayer—because if one confesses, it is hoped that one is forgiven."

The matador's tale became a viral Internet phenomenon, a new kind of modern myth. It swept through social media like wildfire, heating up a conversation about what it would take to walk away from such a big life, on a very big stage.

The only problem is that the story isn't true.

Not long after it broke, it was revealed to be a hoax, more accurately an embellishment. In actuality, Builes didn't walk away from the bull in the middle of a fight. Instead, on that September day in 1984, it was the bull that put a stop to Builes's career. The bull caught him in the foot and tossed him across the ring like a rag doll. Builes sustained a neck fracture of the cervical vertebrae that left him a paraplegic.

Gradually, as he recuperated and began to acclimate to his new life, Builes experienced a slow conversion. Despite the catastrophic injury that left him permanently confined to a wheelchair, it was remorse for the pain and suffering he had caused the animals that led to a new way of doing and being. Out of a past that included both victory and failure, the former matador emerged as someone altogether new. He became a leading activist in the charge to ban bullfighting.

Although the version of the story that captured the attention of so many was a distortion, the reasons it struck a chord far outshine the lie. The embellished story speaks to something true and beautiful that is alive in every human being. It points to a longing for a different kind of hero—one who can demonstrate the courage required to break free of a life inauthentic; who leaves a map of inspiration for others on their way to exploring the uncharted path.

That said, the real story is even more intricate and layered than the viral version. For Builes, what came after his life-changing injury was the challenge to re-create himself. He was able to do that not by renouncing his skills, talents, and gifts; nor by denying the mastery he had attained. None of that was lost. All that had come before made him uniquely qualified to pursue his real work.

It is not always pleasurable to get real . . . or to find our real work. Sometimes you have to confront painful truths. But if you resist The Most Amazing Thing when the whole of your being is longing for it, then you set yourself up to create ever more difficult challenges. There is good reason for this:

Your creative self will not be denied.

The good news is that if you pay attention to it, then it does not have to be difficult. El Pilar's story reminds us that The Most Amazing Thing is always close at hand. You just have to dig for it.

Creators know to dig for it.

*Your creative self will not be denied.*

# *Try This!*

## THE ULTRACREATIVE WALKABOUT—
## WHEN SEEKING DIRECTION AND GUIDANCE

I recently finished a movie script where the heroine has to travel a great distance across Europe all alone, and she is being chased by a band of incredibly nasty guys. Whenever she gets lost, she makes a map for herself with a piece of soft leather that she wears as a bandanna. She wets the leather and lays it out in the sun to dry. When it is completely dry, she smoothens it and looks at the crisscrossed wrinkles and lines—all of which become the topography of her map.

When seeking guidance she asks the map, "Which way do I go now?" Whichever line on her map makes itself known as the next step, she follows with courage and with faith. And the outcome works out surprisingly well.

You, too, can design this kind of intuitive map and go on an ultracreative walkabout of your own making.

- *Choose an inquiry or issue to hold in your heart.* It is this inquiry that aligns your ultracreative self with your allies and cocreators. It aligns you with your subconscious mind, the muses, and any other unseen friends and guides you may be working with.
- *Find a tool to provide feedback.* In my story, the heroine uses her leather bandanna, but you could use almost anything. Two ideas: arbitrarily pick a page in a book and read the third paragraph, or open a magazine to page 44 and refer to the first image or word you see.

Receive the information and act:

183

- Your task is to figure out the answer to your question—from the feedback and clues that you receive—and then to follow that answer. Trust it. Take action with courage and faith.

# CHAPTER 18
# *Your Life as Art*

*Go forth into the busy world and love it. Interest yourself in its life,*
*mingle kindly with its joys and sorrows.*
—RALPH WALDO EMERSON

The fox in Aesop's fable slinks around the perimeter of the vineyard. She can see and smell the most succulent grapes. There are thousands of these bite-sized treats. But there is one problem: a large stone wall separating her from the grapes. She can overcome this obstacle, she is sure of it. So she takes a mighty leap.

She doesn't make it.

She tries again.

And again and again and again.

She wants those grapes. She can taste those grapes. *They are going to be so delicious!*

After a time, the fox gets discouraged and gives up. But just before she trots off, she finds a way to come to terms with her shortcomings and failings.

"Those grapes were sour anyway!" she declares to the wind.

With that, she walks away.

The fox decided that if she couldn't be all-creative, she would make up for it by being all-knowing—omniscient. She decided that she *knew* something about the grapes that would relieve her of the burden of what she saw as failure.

Something happens right *there*.

We set out to fulfill a desire—to innovate a dream or create something that is an expression of who we are. And if it doesn't come to pass—if we "fail"—we can go to the familiar attitudes, beliefs, thoughts, and feelings that give us some temporary comfort or relief. We must *always* create, so we create a hand-me-down condition or story to explain and justify the outcome. We settle. We create our reasons to stay small.

The fox could have made other choices. She could have cobbled together a ramp. She could have climbed a tree growing next to the wall. She could have found an entirely different vineyard to satisfy her craving. She could have lingered in the awkward discomfort of not knowing how it would play out. But she chose, too soon, to discharge her creative impulse.

We know that living creatively won't come from remaining loyal to hand-me-down approaches to life, work, and love. It won't suffice to repeat the past, or mimic others who appear to have cracked the creative code, tracing the lines they have already drawn.

In order for us to have a relationship with innovation and inspiration, there comes a time when we can no longer settle for a life that is simply an improvement over what *was*. What we want—what calls to us—is beyond the horizon of what *is*. Creating that life and opening to it isn't a matter of cataloguing accomplishments and acquiring information. It has more to do with a particular quality of knowledge.

> *In order for us to have a relationship with innovation and inspiration, there comes a time when we can no longer settle for a life that is simply an improvement over what was.*

## DILIGENCE AND DEVOTION— THE PATH OF MASTERY

In my teens, when I attended film school in London, I learned that the cabbies in London had to gain what they called "the knowledge." They would walk the city, day after day for a couple of years, before they even began to drive it. They would make notes on the main routes, all 320 of them involving some 25,000 streets. This blew my mind. Eventually they would track every mile of the city on a scooter, still long before getting behind the wheel of a taxicab. In total, it would take close to three years of diligence to gain the skill and intimate knowledge required for licensing. They would become not simply artisans of the territory but *artists* of the territory.

This tradition, the making of a London cabbie, is still happening today. In many ways, it epitomizes the creative life. First comes the drudge work, the attention to detail, the practice, the obstruction, the willingness and courage to act even when obstruction is strong; and then some measure of mastery is achieved.

For the drivers, an intricate weave of details goes into the creation of the most efficient route from point A to point B: traffic patterns, location of roundabouts, schedule of public events, weather conditions, road repairs, and all the points of interest along the way. It's quite magical. Having tended to every mile, they are no longer hesitant. They can move from point of origin to destination with the least amount of fuss necessary. They reference no maps or navigation systems. It starts as an assembling of details, and then all of a sudden there is an alchemical shift. This vast amount of information is distilled. The cabby swallows it, in a sense, and the body of knowledge is integrated. A genius comes forth that masterfully coordinates an extraordinary relationship with a place and the people who travel it. Vocation becomes exploration.

As a creator, when integration happens—when the work you love, your creative expression, the way you contribute all become second nature—you have mastery. Fully absorbed in your subconscious, *the knowledge* is now in the body. You own it. From that place, creative solutions arise spontaneously. You learn to hold strategies and plans lightly and to *respond* more. Right action, as the Buddhists say, becomes instinctive. At some point, the mastery is so elegant—there is so little energy expended for such tremendous impact—that it becomes invisible. What was, once upon a time, a struggle is now seamless. Doing and being merge into one creative force.

There is no longer a distinction between what is and isn't creative. You know in your body that every act is a creative act. Everything you love is a confluence of creative acts.

> *When integration happens—when the work you love, your creative expression, the way you contribute all become second nature—you have mastery.*

## THE VIRTUOUS LOOP

It could be that enlightenment itself is the discovery that *life is a creative act*, and the world in which we move is a feedback system of our own creativity.

It all becomes a virtuous loop of energy: We engage in creative practices. The creative practices increase our bandwidth, expanding our abilities to notice, sense, and see. Paying more attention, we notice where and when something feels a little bit different, where there is feedback, however subtle or small. We consciously endow the feedback we receive with meaning. And as we endow the feedback with meaning, our subconscious gets the message: "More of this!"

In essence, the virtuous loop is a map of the self as Creator, wherein we recognize ourselves created by the world in which we live, at the same time we are creating it.

## METAPHOR AND MEANING

Poets practice decoding reality as if the world of experience is loaded with significance, as indeed it is. Likewise, the creator does not stop at the surface of things but always looks more deeply, searching for and expecting to find the meaning of things. Walking down a city street, rambling through a field, picking up a rock, running into an old friend, encountering a challenge—we're not separate from these. We begin to see them through the poet's eyes. We approach our lives, the world, and every circumstance and situation as a metaphor for our creative self.

When everything that occurs is grist for the mill, conjuring up and expressing a deeper set of meanings, the entire world becomes an enchanted place, a feedback system delivering ever-deeper understandings.

This is the culminating gift of creativity: greater intimacy with all life in and around you.

> *When everything that occurs is grist for the mill,*
> *conjuring up and expressing a deeper set of meanings,*
> *the entire world becomes an enchanted place.*

## THE ARTISTRY OF RELATIONSHIPS

Creating and giving back, creating and giving back—around and around in a virtuous loop of relationship. Although periods of solitude and self-reflection are essential, the creative life doesn't happen in a vacuum. London cabbies don't acquire *the knowledge* alone. To rise to the rigors of their calling, to become artists of their domain, they must rely on the city—for guidance, input, course correcting, inspiration, and friendship. The same is true for all creators. Busting through conditioning and complacency requires personal attention and diligence, and it also requires receiving. It is a cha-cha-cha of doing and being. From solving big problems to seizing big opportunities, we were never meant to go it alone.

## FALLING IN LOVING WITH THE DANCE

Like any skill, learning the cha-cha-cha requires discipline and devotion. To become a skilled creator, you have to fall in love with the cha-cha-cha, with the dance of doing and being. You open to what is possible when the capacities of will and action come together with imagination, feeling, and being. Then rather than sitting on the sidelines, you become a partner with the energy and rhythm of the life that moves through you.

That's when the magic happens.

You suddenly have a greater capacity to perceive and conceive of the life you want to live, beyond validation and approval. You stop being created by your past and start consciously creating your present and future. When you have sufficient tools, practices, and rituals to embody and express your vision, when you have adequately individuated from the programming and conditioning of your upbringing, the whole of your life becomes an act of creation—your creation.

Your life becomes art.

## LET GO

I have one more story to share with you.

There was an old man working in the elephant pen at the circus. He had been doing the job for more than forty years, and every night he cried about his wretched life. He complained bitterly. His back ached. His feet hurt. His hands were stiff. His hair and clothing reeked of stale hay and elephant dung. He was sick and tired of hearing the sound of his own voice as he talked to beasts that couldn't talk back.

One day his wife had enough. "Why don't you try something new?" she said.

He was incredulous. He looked up from his plate at his wife and said, "What—? And get out of show business?!"

Like the elephant keeper, sometimes we won't let go—of a job, an identity, a way of being or relating—even when life is difficult and full of complaints. We won't let go because it is what we know. As much as we want to be free of circumstances that have sprung up from our structured imaginations, there are also payoffs in them. And the fear of what we could lose can be greater than where we believe creativity can lead us.

I know these fears intimately. I also know this: Creativity is a gift. If you open to creativity, she will come for you. She will take you on the ride of your life.

Be brave.

# ACKNOWLEDGMENTS

I am deeply indebted to my masterly editors, Debra Evans and Leslie Meredith, who took my rambling words and incomplete thoughts and made me look like a man of letters. You deepened every page of this book. Thank you.

I am grateful to my publisher, Judith Curr and the team at Atria Books, for giving me this platform. Finally, I would like to express my immense appreciation to my dear friends and teachers. You prove that creativity can be taught.

# Index

## INDEX

# ABOUT THE AUTHOR

Barnet Bain is an award-winning motion picture producer and director, radio broadcaster, and creativity expert. Select film credits include Academy Award–winner *What Dreams May Come* (producer); Prime-time Emmy Award nominee for Outstanding Made for Television Movie *Homeless to Harvard* (executive producer); *The Celestine Prophecy* (screenwriter, producer); *The Jesus Film* (screenwriter); and *The Lost and Found Family* (director).

Barnet is cohost of Cutting Edge Consciousness, a radio show and podcast series offering a fresh format for experiencing many of today's visionary leaders and thinkers in "kitchen table"–style conversations.

Barnet consults and trains business leaders and private clients who are committed to high performance. Through his workshops and training seminars, Barnet guides people of all ages to expand their vision of what is possible, and to contribute their gifts and talents with passion.

**FOR MORE INFORMATION:**
www.barnetbain.com
www.cuttingedgeconsciousness.com